LANCHESTER LIBRARY

WITHDRAWN

3 8001 00260 5883

£25.00

KT-584-702

Coventry

The physiological basis of behaviour

During this century huge technological advances have improved the methodologies available to the neuroscientist. In this clear and accessible introductory text, Kevin Silber introduces us to the methods of investigating brain function, examines the central nervous system, the autonomic nervous system and the endocrine system, and considers homeostasis as an example of how the central nervous system and the autonomic nervous system work together. He concludes with a discussion of how drugs affect the brain.

The Physiological Basis of Behaviour is tailor-made for the student new to higher-level study, covering all the basic concepts needed in this area of bio-psychology, with helpful textbook features to assist in examination and learning techniques.

Kevin Silber is Senior Lecturer in Psychology at Staffordshire University and an experienced examiner at A level.

Routledge Modular Psychology

Series editors: Cara Flanagan is the Assessor for the Associated Examining Board (AEB) and an experienced A-level author. Kevin Silber is Senior Lecturer in Psychology at Staffordshire University. Both are A-level examiners in the UK.

The *Routledge Modular Psychology* series is a completely new approach to introductory level psychology, tailor-made to the new modular style of teaching. Each short book covers a topic in more detail than any large textbook can, allowing teacher and student to select material exactly to suit any particular course or project.

The books have been written especially for those students new to higher-level study, whether at school, college or university. They include specially designed features to help with technique, such as a model essay at an average level with an examiner's comments to show how extra marks can be gained. The authors are all examiners and teachers at the introductory level.

The *Routledge Modular Psychology* texts are all user-friendly and accessible and include the following features:

- practice essays with specialist commentary to show how to achieve a higher grade
- chapter summaries to assist with revision
- progress and review exercises
- glossary of key terms
- summaries of key research
- further reading to stimulate ongoing study and research
- website addresses for additional information
- cross-referencing to other books in the series

Also available in this series (titles listed by syllabus section):

The physiological basis of behaviour
Neural and hormonal processes

Kevin Silber

London and New York

Coventry University

First published 1999
by Routledge
11 New Fetter Lane, London EC4P 4EE

Simultaneously published in the USA and Canada
by Routledge
29 West 35th Street, New York, NY 10001

© 1999 Kevin Silber

Typeset inTimes by Routledge
Printed and bound in Great Britain by Clays Ltd, St Ives plc

All rights reserved. No part of this book may be reprinted or
reproduced or utilised in any form or by any electronic, mechanical,
or other means, now known or hereafter invented, including
photocopying and recording, or in any information storage or
retrieval system, without permission in writing from the publishers.

British Library Cataloguing in Publication Data
A catalogue record for this book is available from the British Library

Library of Congress Cataloging in Publication Data
Silber, Kevin, 1959–
The physiological basis of behaviour: neural and hormonal processes / Kevin Silber.
p. cm – (Routledge modular psychology; 1).
Includes bibliographical references and index.
1. Psychophysiology.
2. Brain–Effect of drugs on.
I. Title
II. Series.
QP360.S49 1999
612.8–dc21   98–33671

ISBN 0–415–18653–6 (hbk)
ISBN 0–415–18654–4 (pbk)

To Susan, Jonathan, Dominic and Anna-Liese

Contents

Illustrations

Figures

Tables

Acknowledgements

The series editors and Routledge acknowledge the expert help of Paul Humphreys, Examiner and Reviser for A-level Psychology, in compiling the Study Aids section of each book in the series.

They also acknowledge the Associated Examining Board (AEB) for granting permission to use their examination material. The AEB do not accept responsibility for the answers or examiner comment in the Study Aids section of this book or any other book in the series.

Methods of investigating brain function

Introduction

Gaining knowledge about the workings of the brain is not an easy task. In the early part of the twentieth century, neuroanatomists relied on a keen eye and a little help from the **light microscope**. However, during this century huge technological advances have improved the methodologies available to the neuroscientist. In this chapter we will explore some of these methodologies and evaluate their contribution to our knowledge.

The chapter is divided into two parts: neuroanatomical techniques, which allow us to learn more about the structure of the brain; and neurophysiological techniques, which allow us to investigate the functioning of the brain.

Neuroanatomical techniques

There are a number of different techniques which allow neuroanatomists to investigate the structure of the brain. These range from simple observations using microscopes, to chemical staining methods allowing us to pinpoint nerve cells and fibre pathways, to brain scanning techniques that allow us to construct 3D images of the whole brain.

Electron microscopy

Rationale

This method allows us to see in detail the size and shape of neurons and their components (Figure 1.1).

Description

The **electron microscope** uses electrons instead of light to magnify the image. This allows us to see actual synapses which are only a few ten-millionths of a millimetre in diameter. (The unit which represents one ten-millionth of a millimetre is the angstrom which has the symbol Å.) Another type of electron microscope is the scanning electron microscope, which lets us see the image in 3D, although the magnification has to be very slightly reduced.

Electron microscopy is used routinely today to examine changes in the structure of neurons either after brain damage or in response to **information processing**. For example, Spinelli *et al.* (1980) showed that the structure of neurons in a sensory area of a kitten's brain changed after it had learned a simple **conditioning** task.

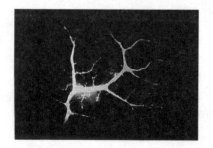

Figure 1.1 **An electron photomicrograph of a neuron**

Evaluation

This method gives us a very clear picture of the minute detail of neurons. However, the equipment is extremely expensive and the method can only be used post mortem.

Chemical staining

Rationale

Staining methods allow us to trace the extent of features of the nervous system. For example, we can examine where cell bodies are or search for where the neurons from a particular region of the brain project to. There are a vast number of different stains that can be applied to brain tissue sections and each has a different feature that it highlights best.

Description

To stain brain tissue a small slice is usually mounted on a microscope slide and then dipped in the staining fluid. The slide is then viewed under a light microscope. Figure 1.2 shows a photograph of a section of rat's brain stained to reveal cell bodies. It is also possible to stain large sections of brain so that the fibre pathways from one region to another can be traced.

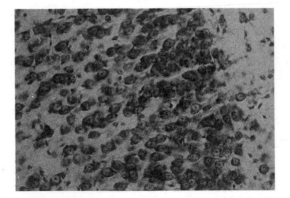

Figure 1.2 **Stained cell bodies of neurons in the brain**

Evaluation

This method has the advantage that most of the stains are colour. This means that particular components can be highlighted and more easily seen against the background of other components. A disadvantage of this method is that the process of staining is slow and can be very costly. Also, stains cannot provide an accurate picture as not all of a particular component will stain fully. So, for example, one might be able to see where a type of cell body is concentrated but one couldn't measure the precise density using this method. As with electron microscopy, this method can only be used post mortem.

Brain scans

Rationale

Brain imaging allows us to create pictures of a slice through the whole, living brain. Some types of scan allow for 3D images of the brain to be built up. Others allow us to get a picture of active and passive brain regions during the performance of a task.

Description

There are basically three different types of brain scan. **Computerised axial tomography (CAT or CT)** scans pass X-rays through the head and record sections of the brain. A series of sections can be taken to give a 3D representation of the brain. **Magnetic resonance imaging (MRI)** scans are similar to CT scans but instead of using X-rays they use magnetic fields. This gives a slightly clearer picture. Finally, **positron emission tomography (PET)** scans let us see the activity of the brain. The patient is first given an injection of a mildly radioactive form of glucose and is then put in the scanner. As those regions of the brain that are active will be using more sugar for energy, these regions will use the radioactive sugar. This radioactivity is detected by the scanner and so the active regions show up on the picture. These scanning techniques represent the major recent advance in neuroscientific investigation. They have been used, for example, to detect brain damage in certain areas of the brains of Alzheimer's patients (Jobst 1992).

Evaluation

This method has been a major breakthrough for researchers trying to understand the workings of the normal brain and for clinicians trying to detect brain abnormalities such as tumours. The scans can also help the brain surgeon to decide whether or not surgery is necessary. The main advantage is that this is the only set of neuroanatomical methods that allow analysis in a living organism. One small disadvantage is that the machinery used to take the scans is very imposing and a few patients find the experience too traumatic (a feeling of claustrophobia is quite common). In addition, as with other methods, brain scans are very expensive to carry out.

Which of the techniques described so far would best be suited to investigating the following scenarios. For each scenario state the best technique and say why it would be better than the others.

1 You wish to investigate where the fibres (axons) of the hippocampus project to.
2 A patient presents with a suspected brain tumour.
3 You are investigating the structure of the terminal bouton.
4 A patient complains of reading difficulties and you wish to investigate whether a language centre of the brain is dysfunctional (i.e. not working properly).

Progress exercise

Neurophysiological techniques

There are several methods that allow neuroscientists to investigate how the brain works. The neuroscientist can do one of four things to investigate function. S/he can destroy part of the brain to see how the organism manages without that part of the brain (lesioning), s/he can stimulate a part of the brain to see what behaviour occurs, s/he can record from the brain to measure the activity taking place, or s/he can inject chemicals into the brain and look at the changes in behaviour that occur.

Lesioning

Rationale

By removing a part of the brain the neuroscientist can investigate that part's function. This method can be used to test whether an area performs a particular function. It can also be used to see if an area is necessary for a function to develop. The area removed can be as small as a few millimetres in diameter or can be as large as a whole structure.

Description

Lesions are made under anaesthesia by inserting an electrode into the brain and passing a small electric current through it. The tissue around the electrode is destroyed either by the electric current itself or by the heat produced at the electrode. The size of the current determines the size of the lesion.

One example of a lesion study is by Jouvet and Renault (1966). They lesioned, in cats, an area of the brain called the **raphe system** and found that the cat would remain awake for a day or more. This led them to suspect that the raphe system might have a role to play in initiating sleep.

Evaluation

Lesions are very useful in helping to determine the functions of brain areas. However, care needs to be taken when interpreting the results from lesion studies. Any **functional deficit** may not be due to the region removed. Instead it might be because the lesion has disrupted the supply of information to that area or the supply of information from that area to another area. Another caution comes when no deficit is found after a lesion. Another, undamaged area may also (be able to) carry out the function normally reserved for the lesioned area.

Brain stimulation

Rationale

By stimulating a region of the brain it is possible to try to initiate certain behaviours and thereby learn what function(s) that region of the brain controls.

Description

Stimulation electrodes can be lowered through a small hole made in the skull. The small amount of electricity passed through is insufficient to do any damage but will stimulate the neurons in the region to fire. An example of where this has been used is to investigate pleasure centres in the brain. If a stimulating electrode is placed in an area of a rat's **limbic system** it has been found that the rat will press a lever repeatedly in order to receive the stimulation (it obviously likes it). In fact the rat will keep pressing the lever very fast (around 2,000 times per hour) until it eventually collapses from exhaustion (Olds 1958).

Evaluation

This method has only limited uses because the electrode causes all of the neurons in the stimulated region to fire. We cannot be sure whether under normal circumstances all of the local neurons would be firing at the same time. Nevertheless, this method can provide pointers to the sort of information that a region processes.

Recording methods

Rationale

The purpose of recording techniques is to read the brain activity that is occurring when an organism does something. Recording can be at the gross level using scalp electrodes or can be the firing of a single neuron using microelectrodes. Scalp electrodes are used to record the activity of large regions of the brain such as the whole of the left hemisphere. **Microelectrodes** can tell us whether a single neuron is involved in a particular process such as single cells in the **visual cortex**.

Description

Scalp electrodes record **electroencephalographic (EEG)** activity from the surface of the head. They can detect things like hemispheric differences. For example, when reading, the left hemisphere is more active than the right as this is where language processing takes place. The EEG can also be used to measure levels of sleep or wakefulness (Dement and Kleitman 1957).

Microelectrodes come in two sorts. One type are about 150 μm (microns or micrometres – a micron is one millionth of a metre) in diameter (about as thick as a human hair); these are used to record **multiple unit activity (MUA)**. This is the processing activity of a few hundred neurons, the recording taken from the extracellular fluid surrounding the neurons. This type of recording enabled Hubel and Wiesel (1977) to discover the responses of different parts of the visual cortex to features of a visual stimulus.

The other type of microelectrode is no more than 50 μm in diameter and is used to record **single unit activity (SUA)**. This is the processing activity from just one neuron, the recording taken from the intracellular fluid inside the neuron. Berger *et al.* (1986) have shown that the activity of single neurons in the **hippocampus** correlates almost perfectly with the learning of a conditioned response in the rabbit.

Evaluation

In general, recording electrodes have given us a lot of information about the way in which the brain processes information. The disadvantage of scalp electrodes is that they are limited in what they can tell you as the recording is from such a large area. The disadvantage of MUA is that you might be recording from neurons that have different functions but which all reside in the same small area. Whilst SUA is by far the most useful type of information, this method is extremely difficult to carry out. Neurons are so small that if the organism moves the electrode could be dislodged from its position. Thus SUA can usually only be carried out for a few minutes at a time and the organism has to be relatively immobile.

Neurochemical methods

Rationale

Chemicals can be injected into the brain either to modify or to mimic the actions of neurons. The amount of chemical injected can be large enough to affect much or all of the brain or the amount can be so tiny as to affect just a few cells. By altering or mimicking normal activity, much can be learned about the way in which the brain functions.

Description

Large amounts of a chemical can be injected into the brain via the blood supply provided that the chemical will pass the **blood–brain**

barrier (a filter to protect the brain from harmful substances). Where a chemical will not pass the blood–brain barrier it is sometimes possible to inject a substance that will pass the barrier and then be converted into the wanted chemical once inside the brain. This is the basis upon which many drug treatments for brain disorders are administered. For example, administering dopamine can alleviate the symptoms of **Parkinson's disease** but, because dopamine will not pass the blood–brain barrier, L-DOPA is given instead. The L-DOPA passes through the blood–brain barrier and is then converted into dopamine once inside the brain.

If the blood–brain barrier cannot be overcome by injecting into the blood stream then a pipette can be used to inject the chemical directly into the brain. If tiny quantities are required then a **micropipette** can be used. These are usually made of glass and can have a tip diameter of just a few microns. This technique gives the neuroscientist a very fine control with which to investigate the detailed chemistry of the brain.

Evaluation

The use of large quantities of a chemical for the drug treatment of psychological disorders has had a major impact on the lives of those affected. Indeed, this area is the subject of Chapters 8 and 9. The use of tiny quantities has allowed neuroscientists to investigate the mechanisms by which synapses function. The difficulty of this kind of investigation is that the mechanisms are so complex that finding the correct chemicals and the correct amounts to inject is a major drawback to progress.

Chapter summary

In this chapter we have looked at a number of techniques for investigating the structure and function of the brain. Some techniques, like scans and EEG, allow us to look at whole brain features whereas other techniques, like the electron microscope and single unit activity, allow us to investigate the detail of what the brain looks like and how it works. It is through a combination of these techniques that we come to get a more complete picture of brain functioning. In the rest of the book we will explore the basic neural and hormonal processes that have been revealed using this multiple approach to neuroscience.

Review exercise

Imagine you are one of a group of aliens sent to Earth to learn about the human brain and armed with the techniques described in this chapter. Together the group has roughly determined its gross structural features and you have been assigned to learn as much as you can about what we call the cerebral cortex. Which techniques might you use and what might they reveal?

When you have completed the exercise go back over the chapter and see whether there were any techniques that you missed.

Further reading

Carlson, N.R. (1998) *Physiology of Behaviour*. 6th edn. Allyn & Bacon, Boston, MA. Chapter 5. ISBN 0–205–27340–8. This is a very good general text. Whilst some of the material in this book is qute advanced, the chapter on methods is thorough and easy to follow.

Associated with this text is an Internet on-line study guide which can be found at http://www.abacon.com/carlsonpob

The neuron

Introduction

In everyday language we talk about **nerves** as though each were a single unit of the nervous system. This is not, in fact, the case. A nerve, or **nerve fibre**, is a collection of a large number of more basic units called **neurons**. For example, the nerve that supplies the little finger with movement is made up of many *hundreds* of neurons. In this chapter we will explore what a neuron consists of and how it functions.

The structure of the neuron

Figure 2.1 shows the structure of a typical neuron. The **cell body** has a number of projections from it called **dendrites**. These are the input areas to the neuron. It is through the dendrites that the neuron

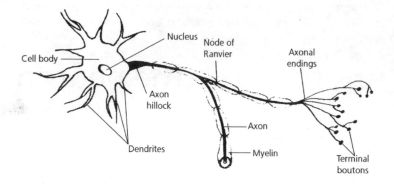

Figure 2.1 **Schematic drawing of a neuron**

receives information from other neurons. Within the cell body is the **nucleus** which contains the DNA (the genetic material that contains the unique coding for our body). Also emerging from the cell body is a long thin projection called the **axon**. This is the output side of the neuron. Note how it is covered along most of its length by a protective coating called **myelin**. Note, also, that the myelin is not continuous but has breaks along its length. These breaks are called **nodes of Ranvier**, named so after their discoverer. The **myelin sheath** serves to protect the axon and also serves to speed up the sending of messages along its length. The axon carries information to other cells. These may be other neurons or they may be **end organs** such as muscles or glands. Along its length the axon may or may not divide into different arms, allowing the information from one neuron to be sent to a number of different places (a property known as **divergence**). At its end(s), it branches into a number of **axonal endings**. At the tip of each axonal ending is a swelling called a **terminal bouton**. Within the terminal bouton are a number of sacs called **vesicles**, which store and release chemicals called **neurotransmitters**. These chemicals are the means by which a neuron communicates with other cells and we shall look at this in more detail shortly. Finally, where the axon leaves the cell body it is thicker than elsewhere along its length. This thicker region is called the **axon hillock**. As we shall see, this is an important region in determining whether or not the neuron passes on any information.

The above description is of a typical neuron but there are neurons of other shapes and structures as well (about thirty in all). In addition, the lengths of our neurons vary enormously from a few microns long such as those in our brains to several feet, such as the ones that enable us to wiggle our toes.

The neuronal membrane

Surrounding the neuron there is a wall called the **neuronal membrane**. Although only a few microns thick, it separates the fluid inside the neuron (the **cytoplasm**) from the fluid outside (the **extracellular fluid**). The membrane is said to be **semi-permeable**, which means that it lets some things pass through it but not others. Generally, smaller things get through the membrane more easily than larger ones. However, the things that can pass through it change depending upon the current state that the neuron is in. The membrane, therefore, plays a very important part in the workings of the neuron.

The resting membrane potential

Now that you know what a neuron looks like and have been introduced to its semi-permeable membrane, we can start to examine how it carries and processes information. To simplify the process let us use the analogy of a piece of wire. A wire always has the potential (called a voltage) to carry electricity; it can either be carrying electricity (live) or not carrying electricity (unlive). In a similar way, a neuron always has the potential (also called a voltage) to carry a message and can either be carrying a message (active) or not carrying a message (resting). We can measure this potential. When the neuron is resting it is called the **resting membrane potential**. In a wire this voltage is measured as the difference between the potential at the point of measurement and the earth (which has zero potential). In a neuron the voltage is measured as the difference in potential between the inside of the neuron and the outside (i.e. the potential across the neuronal membrane).

To continue the wire analogy for a moment, a wire carries electricity by passing a charge along its length. This is true also of a neuron. However, in a neuron the charge is made by things called **ions**, atoms that carry an electrical charge. Hence the resting membrane potential is measured as the difference between the charge due to ions inside the neuron and the charge due to ions outside the neuron. Figure 2.2 shows the important ions that are involved in creating the resting membrane potential. As you can see, sodium and potassium ions (both positively charged) exist on both sides of the membrane. However, much more sodium lies outside the neuron than inside (hence the large and small letters). The opposite is true for potassium. Of the negatively charged protein ions (not shown in Figure 2.2), there are none on the outside. The net effect of this balance of ions is to create a potential difference of **−70 millivolts** (usually written as −70 mV). The minus sign indicates that the inside of the neuron is negative with respect to the outside.

The action potential

When a neuron is sending a message down its axon it is said to be carrying an **action potential**. Another way to say this is to state that the neuron is **firing**. What exactly does this mean? You will remember that the neuronal membrane is semi-permeable. Under certain conditions, the membrane becomes more permeable (i.e. leaky), first to sodium ions and then to potassium ions. It might help to think of sodium and potassium gates being opened and closed. When the gates are closed to an ion the membrane is virtually leakproof, and when it is open to an ion the membrane is extremely leaky. Only when the gate is open can ions move freely across the membrane. When the membrane becomes more permeable to sodium ions, those ions on the outside of the neuron flood inside in much the same way as water floods through a dam that has burst. This is because there are far more sodium ions outside than there are inside. When the ions flood in they change the

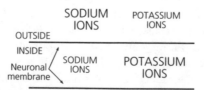

Figure 2.2 **Ion distribution across the neuronal membrane**

Note: The greater the size of lettering, the larger the number of ions

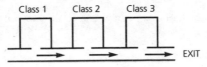

Figure 2.3 Analogy of the flow of an action potential down an axon

membrane potential, making it alter from −70 mV to around +40 mV. Just before the potential reaches +40 mV, the increased permeability to sodium ceases and the membrane becomes more permeable to potassium. As there are more potassium ions inside the neuron than outside they flood out. This brings the membrane potential back to where it started at −70 mV.

The action potential starts at the axon hillock (if the threshold potential is reached) and progresses down the axon until it reaches the terminal boutons. A simple analogy will show you why it only moves in one direction (from axon hillock to terminal boutons). Figure 2.3 shows three classrooms which open onto a narrow corridor. At the end of the corridor is the exit from the school. Imagine it is 3.00 p.m. and the fifty pupils of class 1 are allowed to go home. They flood into the corridor and make their way to the exit. At the same time the fifty pupils in class 2 are allowed out. When they enter the narrow corridor they have little chance of walking towards class 1 even if they wanted to. They rush towards the exit trying to prevent being stampeded by the oncoming pupils of class 1. The same is true for the fifty pupils of class 3 who are also allowed out at the same time. As you can see, there is only one direction of momentum possible and the same sort of process is true for ions entering the neuron anywhere along its membrane.

You may now be wondering what the nodes of Ranvier are for. Most neurons are covered with a myelin sheath which does not allow ions to cross the membrane. The nodes of Ranvier provide periodic gaps at which the movement of ions across the membrane can occur.

Progress exercise

See if you can define the following terms without having to refer back to previous pages.

Action potential
Axon
Dendrite
End organ
Ion
Myelin
Nerve
Resting membrane potential
Vesicle

Now go back to the text and see if you were correct.

Neurotransmitters

We have now covered the activity of the neuron until the action potential reaches the terminal boutons. From here the process moves from an electrochemical one to a purely chemical one. The connection between one neuron and the next (or between a neuron and an end organ) is not direct. Instead there is a gap, called the **synaptic cleft**, between them. The way in which messages are transmitted across this gap is via **neurotransmitter substances**.

Figure 2.4 shows a diagram of the inside of a terminal bouton. Within the terminal bouton are sacs called **synaptic vesicles**. These store chemical substances called neurotransmitter substances. When the action potential reaches the terminal bouton a series of events takes place that leads to the neurotransmitter substance being released from the vesicles. The neurotransmitter substance migrates to the tip of the terminal bouton where it is released from the neuron. The mitochondria (the energy providers in the cell) are also shown in Figure 2.4. Before we look at what happens next, let us briefly examine some of the neurotransmitters.

There are a large number of neurotransmitters and Table 2.1 lists a

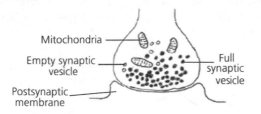

Mitochondria

Empty synaptic vesicle

Postsynaptic membrane

Full synaptic vesicle

Figure 2.4 **Diagram of a terminal bouton**

few of the most psychologically important ones. You will meet most of these again in later chapters in this book and in the other Biological Psychology books in this series. The three middle ones in Table 2.1 (**noradrenaline**, **serotonin** and **dopamine**) are all members of a single group called the **catecholamines** (also known as the *monoamines*).

As already stated, neurotransmitters are special chemicals which have the ability to communicate the message from one neuron to other neurons or end organs. Some neurotransmitters are **excitatory**. This means that they try to stimulate the next neuron or the end organ. Others are **inhibitory** and try to prevent such stimulation.

As we shall see in the next section, what gives a neurotransmitter its special properties is the shape of its molecule. Because of this, other substances which have a similar shape (but which are not naturally occurring neurotransmitters in our bodies) can fool the receiving neuron into believing that the neurotransmitter is present. If such a substance results in the same effect as the natural neurotransmitter (be that either excitation or inhibition) then the substance is called an

Table 2.1 Important neurotransmitter substances	
Name of neurotransmitter substance	*Tends to be …*
Acetylcholine	excitatory
Noradrenaline	excitatory
Serotonin (5HT)	excitatory
Dopamine	excitatory
GABA	inhibitory

agonist. If the substance prevents the effect of the natural neurotransmitter (be that either excitation or inhibition) then the substance is called an **antagonist**.

Under normal circumstances, the balance between excitation and inhibition is a fine one, and many psychological disorders can be traced to the malfunction of one or other neurotransmitter substance. For example, **schizophrenia** has been linked to too much of the neurotransmitter called dopamine and epilepsy has been linked to too little of the neurotransmitter called GABA.

The synapse

We started this chapter with the anatomy of the neuron and you saw in Figure 2.1 projections from the cell body called dendrites. On the dendrites are tiny regions which lie underneath the terminal boutons of other neurons. The wall of the dendrite at such a point is called the **postsynaptic membrane** (Figure 2.4). Together, the postsynaptic membrane from one neuron, the terminal bouton from the previous neuron and the synaptic cleft between them make up a region called the **synapse**.

When the neurotransmitter substance is released from the terminal bouton of a neuron it flows across the synaptic cleft and lands on special regions of the postsynaptic membrane called **receptors**. These receptors have a special configuration into which only the correctly shaped neurotransmitter molecule will fit. For obvious reasons, this perfect fit has been likened to a lock and key. Once the neurotransmitter substance has linked to a receptor molecule, the semi-permeable membrane becomes more permeable to either sodium ions, potassium ions or chloride ions. If the permeability to sodium ions increases then sodium flows into the neuron thereby exciting it. If, however, the permeability to potassium ions increases, potassium flows out of the neuron thereby inhibiting it. If the permeability to chloride ions increases, they flow into the neuron (like sodium) but, because they are negatively charged, they inhibit it. If the local exchange of ions causes excitation, this is referred to as an excitatory post-synaptic potential (EPSP). If the local exchange is inhibitory, this is an inhibitory post-synaptic potential (IPSP).

If the neurotransmitter remained attached to the receptor site then the permeability changes would be permanent. Thus the neurotransmitter substance is released from the receptor site after a few milliseconds. However, we now have a situation where released neurotransmitter molecules are in the synaptic cleft. These could reattach to a receptor site and restart the permeability changes. We do not want this to occur as this would no longer indicate that an action potential had occurred (this signal has already been sent). There are two main mechanisms by which the neurotransmitter molecules can be inactivated. The first is by the molecules being reabsorbed into the presynaptic terminal. The second is by the molecules being broken down. For example, acetylcholinesterase breaks down acetylcholine and monoamine oxidase breaks down the monoamine neurotransmitter substances. This breaking down process can occur either in the synaptic cleft or once the molecule has been reabsorbed into the presynaptic terminal. One advantage of breaking these molecules down is that some of the resulting chemicals can be reused to make more neurotransmitter molecules.

Summation

The activity at any one excitatory synapse will not cause the postsynaptic neuron to fire because the amount of excitation is minuscule. However, if lots of excitatory synapses are active simultaneously, the net effect is to cause an action potential in the receiving neuron. Our sequence of events then starts all over again in this postsynaptic neuron. The principle described here, that of simultaneous activity, is called **spatial summation** and is a very important concept in understanding how meaningful information is conveyed around the brain. By way of example, imagine that a postsynaptic neuron is a bird-recognition neuron that only fires if a bird has been seen. Three presynaptic neurons make contact with this neuron. One fires only when a beak is present, one fires only when two legs are present, and the third fires only when feathers are present. It is only when all three presynaptic neurons fire simultaneously that our bird recognition neuron will be sufficiently excited to fire and thereby register the presence of a bird. Although this example is highly simplified, it serves to illustrate how the convergence of messages is vital in order for the brain to process information.

Another way in which a postsynaptic neuron could be sufficiently excited is if a single presynaptic neuron were to fire repeatedly in quick succession. This principle is called **temporal summation** and might be used to register the intensity of a stimulus. However, you should note that such temporal summation is highly unlikely to occur if only one presynaptic neuron is firing.

Together, the combination of excitation and inhibition, along with temporal and spatial summation, provide the nervous system with a powerful means of communicating information. In the next chapter we will examine the means by which we can understand the informational content of these neuronal messages. Once we have done this we will be in a good position to explore some of the ways in which our knowledge helps to explain the psychology of human behaviour.

Autoreceptors

As well as receptor sites on the postsynaptic membrane, there are also receptor sites in the membrane of the terminal bouton. These receptors are called **autoreceptors**. Their purpose is to regulate the amount of neurotransmitter released from the presynaptic terminal. When neurotransmitter is released, some molecules will diffuse to the autoreceptors. These signal to the inside of the presynaptic terminal that there is sufficient neurotransmitter already in the synaptic cleft and so release of further neurotransmitter is inhibited. This is an example of a negative feedback mechanism of which we will meet further examples.

Chapter summary

In this chapter we have explored the structure and functioning of neurons. We have seen how the neuron communicates its information by a combination of electrical and chemical signalling mechanisms. We have also seen how these signals can combine to yield meaningful messages which are used to process information.

The following describes the sequence of events from the axon hillock of an excitatory neuron to the postsynaptic membrane of the next neuron. Some of the words are missing and your task is to fill in the blanks.

When the voltage at the axon hillock reaches the _____ level, an action potential is initiated. If the ____ is myelinated then the action potential jumps from one node of Ranvier to the next, a process called _____ _____. Once the action potential reaches the terminal bouton it causes the _____ substance to be released from its synaptic _____ into the synaptic _____. From here it diffuses across where it locks onto a _____ site on the _____ membrane. This causes a local exchange of ions which gives rise to an ____. These local changes can add together by the processes of _____ and _____ summation.

Now check back through the text to see if you have correctly identified the blanks.

Further reading

Kalat, J.W. (1998) *Biological Psychology*. 6th edn. Brooks/Cole Publishing Company, Belmont, CA. ISBN 0–534–34893–9. An excellent all-round text which deals with this particular section in a lot of detail.

There is an associated internet study centre at:
http://psychstudy.brookscole.com/kalat_bio.shtml
You will need a user-id and password to gain entry to the study centre but this can be obtained by your tutor.

Nicholls, J.G., Martin, A.R. and Wallace, B.G. (1992) *From Neuron to Brain*. 3rd edn. Sinauer Associates, Sunderland, MA. ISBN 0–87893–580–0. This is a slightly higher level text but it might answer more of the questions of the keener student.

Organisation of the central nervous system

Introduction

The reason that psychologists need to know about the workings of the central nervous system is that most, if not all, of our psychological behaviour is underpinned by our physiological makeup (most notably the workings of our brains). Having analysed the neuron, we can now proceed by looking at the structure of our nervous system. In this chapter we will look at the central nervous system and in Chapter 4 we will look at the autonomic nervous system. You may be thinking, why not look at all of it together? Well, the central nervous system is the most important part of our nervous system (the central processing unit, for the computer literate) and is involved in all psychological activity, whereas the autonomic nervous system is a peripheral system and has a specialist function as far as psychological interest is concerned. They are separated here to emphasise their differential importance in biological psychology.

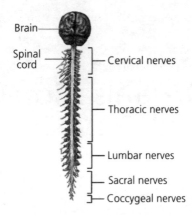

Figure 3.1 **The brain and spinal cord**

In this chapter you will be introduced to a number of brain structures with long, Latin names. Do not be discouraged by this,
especially if this area is totally new to you. Whilst you should not
expect to remember them all on a first reading, you will be amazed at
how quickly you become familiar with the language of biology. You
will also be presented with a number of diagrams showing the layout
of our brains. You should treat these as a road map of the inside of
our skulls. Different angles will be presented to help you to build up a
3D picture of the brain. These will probably be a little confusing at
first but you will soon get the hang of them.

Divisions of the mammalian nervous system

Before we look in detail at the **central nervous system (CNS)**, it is
useful to place it in the context of the entire nervous system. The
mammalian nervous system consists of two components, the CNS
and the **peripheral nervous system (PNS)**. The CNS (Figure 3.1) is
made up of the brain and **spinal cord**. The PNS is further subdivided
into two parts, the **somatic nervous system** and the **autonomic nervous
system (ANS)**. The PNS is connected to the CNS and most of these
connections are made via the spinal cord. The somatic nervous system
consists of nerves that serve the muscles and sensory receptors, and

the ANS is made up of nerves that serve the smooth muscles of the viscera.

As already mentioned, the ANS will be dealt with in Chapter 4. The somatic nervous system will not be dealt with in this book as it has little relevance to psychological behaviour. In the next section we will take a brief look at the **spinal cord**, while the following section will provide a more detailed introduction to the structure of the brain.

The spinal cord

As you can see from Figure 3.1, the spinal cord starts at the base of the brain and runs inside the backbone. On its course it gives off numerous nerves which pass through the gaps between the bones that make up the backbone.

These nerves are grouped into five groups to indicate the regions of the body that they serve. The spinal cord itself is not a single nerve but a collection of different nerves, each with its own function. For example, there are ascending, **afferent**, nerves which carry messages to the brain from peripheral receptors and descending, **efferent**, nerves which carry messages from the brain to muscles, glands, and so on. A good way to think about the spinal cord is as a multi-lane motorway carrying information up and down its length.

We do not need to concern ourselves now with any greater detail concerning the spinal cord. However, as a final word on the subject, the spinal cord carries nerves for both the somatic and autonomic nervous systems and we will need to look more closely at the latter in Chapter 4.

The brain

It is tempting to think of our brain as something solid: in fact, it is anything but. Rose described the brain as 'two fistfuls of pink-grey tissue, wrinkled like a walnut and something of the consistency of porridge...' (1976: 21). To keep this soft organ in place and protected, the brain is covered by a membrane called the **dura mater** and encased in a hard, bony skull.

The human brain is a very complex organ. On its surface you can see a number of folds (Figure 3.2). These are called **sulci** and are there because our brains have outgrown our heads. The surface area of the brain is so large that it would not fit inside our heads unless it was folded up. In fact, two thirds of the surface of the brain lies within these sulci.

We will start our analysis of the brain's structure by looking at how it is divided up. These divisions are based partly on the brain's evolutionary development and partly on the gross anatomical features (the large, easily-defined structures) that were visible with the naked eye to the pioneers of neuroanatomy. However, before we can do this we need to explore, briefly, the terminology used to describe the various planes and directional indicators that are used to locate where in the brain we are referring to (remember that the brain is a three-dimensional structure). This will enable you to orient some of the diagrams that will follow in the rest of the chapter. It might help if you try to think of a human as a four-legged animal rather than a two-legged one. If you imagine the spinal cord extending behind the head then the directional labels become a little more obvious.

Look at Figure 3.3 below as you read each of the following descriptions. Each dimension has a pair of words to describe the two directions along it. **Dorsal/ventral** are used to describe toward the

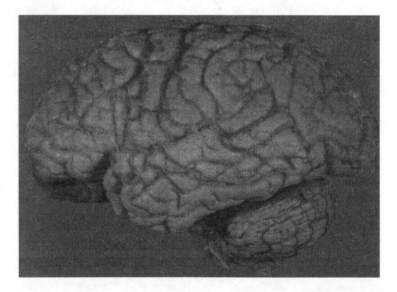

Figure 3.2 **The exterior surface of the brain showing the sulci**

back and toward the front (stomach) respectively. **Anterior/posterior** or **rostral/caudal** describe toward the head end or the rear end. **Medial/lateral** describe toward or away from the midline. For the planes, we have **coronal** describing a slice that goes down from the top of the head and passes through the ears. A **saggital** plane also goes down from the top of the head but this one slices along the line of the nose. Finally, a **horizontal** plane is like slicing the top off an egg.

The brain is divided into three main areas, the **hindbrain**, the **midbrain** and the **forebrain**.

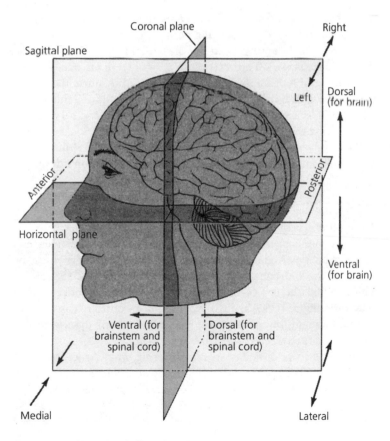

Figure 3.3 **Planes and directional indicators**

Hindbrain

The hindbrain consists of three distinct structures, the **medulla oblongata**, the **pons** and the **cerebellum** (Figure 3.4). The medulla oblongata is situated where the brain meets the spinal cord. It gives rise to many of the cranial nerves which innervate (supply nerves to) the skin and muscles of the face. It controls vital reflexes such as breathing, heart rate, coughing and sneezing. The pons lies anterior to the medulla oblongata and also gives rise to some of the cranial nerves. The word *pons* is Latin for 'bridge' and this name is very appropriate as it is here that many nerve fibres cross over from one side of the midline to the other. Such fibres are referred to as **contralateral** (other side), whilst those that do not cross the midline are called **ipsilateral** (same side). Contained within the medulla and pons are the **raphe nuclei** and most of the **reticular formation** both of which are involved in arousal (see later in this chapter). The cerebellum is situated in an area dorsal to the medulla oblongata and pons. It has two lobes, one either side of the midline, and each lobe has a **cortex** which consists of a thin layer of cells at the surface. The role of the cerebellum is as a control centre for coordinating motor activity. It has become of psychological interest in the last twenty years as researchers have found that it may have a role to play in the learning of some forms of classical conditioning.

Midbrain

The midbrain is quite small in mammals. The anterior part, called the tectum, consists of the **superior colliculus** and **inferior colliculus**, both of which are involved in sensory processing (the former for vision and the latter for audition). The posterior part is called the tegmentum. This contains the rest of the reticular formation (see above) and the **substantia nigra**, which is involved in motor control. It is from the substantia nigra that neurons are lost in Parkinson's disease, leading to the tremors characteristic of this condition.

To add to the difficulty in remembering what structures are in which region, there is another term used to describe the midbrain plus the pons and medulla oblongata. The term is **brainstem** (Figure 3.5), and it is a useful one as it describes all of the regions in the brain which carry out what might be referred to as vital functions (i.e. those

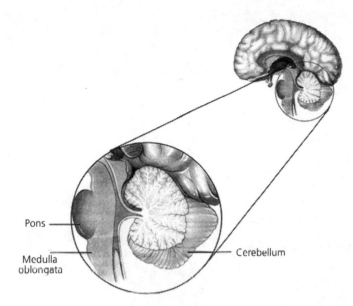

Pons

Medulla
oblongata

Cerebellum

Figure 3.4 **Position of the hindbrain in midline saggital view**

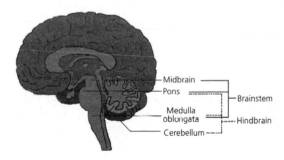

Midbrain
Pons
Medulla
oblongata
Cerebellum

Brainstem
Hindbrain

Figure 3.5 **Saggital section showing brainstem and hindbrain
regions**

Progress exercise

Use the glossary terms at the bottom of this box to fill in the missing words in the following sentences.

A membrane called the _____ covers and protects the brain.

A midline _____ section is a slice that goes between the eyes and down the middle of the nose.

_____ nerves carry outputs from the brain.

The brain and spinal cord make up the _____.

The _____ hypothalamus lies above the ventral hypothalamus.

The _____ are the folds in the cortex of the brain which increase its area.

The words to use are:

CNS	efferent
dorsal	saggital
dura mater	sulci

without which life could not continue). The brainstem is also where 'brain death' is measured from.

Forebrain

The forebrain makes up the largest part of the human brain. In fact, it is so large that it has curled over in order to fit inside our skulls. It is divided into two major regions, the **diencephalon** and the **telencephalon**. It is not possible to describe all of the structures of the forebrain and so we will look only at a few of the more important ones.

Diencephalon

The two most important structures in the diencephalon are the **thalamus** and the **hypothalamus** (Figure 3.6). The thalamus is a major sensory relay station. Almost all sensory information is passed to the thalamus before being sent on to other parts of the forebrain.

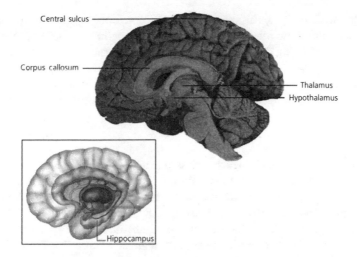

Figure 3.6 **Midline saggital section of subcortical structures with inset showing the 3D positioning of the hippocampus**

Information also comes back to the thalamus from these other brain regions, presumably to control what sensory information gets passed on to the rest of the forebrain. The thalamus is made up of numerous nuclei (collections of cells), each dealing with a different type of sensory information. For example, the lateral geniculate nucleus receives information from the retina of the eye and sends it on to the visual cortex.

The hypothalamus is also made up of a number of nuclei. Its various roles include the control of hunger, thirst, temperature regulation and sexual behaviour. The hypothalamus also controls the **pituitary gland**, which plays a vital role in the control of our hormonal systems.

Telencephalon

The telencephalon is the most important part of our brains as far as higher cognitive functioning (i.e., more elaborate information processing) is concerned. As with the diencephalon, we will concentrate on just a few of the important structures in this region of the brain. The **hippocampus** (Figure 3.6 insert) is a part of a circuit of structures known as the **limbic system** (described later in the chapter).

This structure plays an important role in memory and emotion and mood, amongst other things. The **basal ganglia** is a collection of structures which, along with the cerebellum and the motor cortex, are involved in motor control. The **cerebral cortex** is the most important part of the telencephalon as this is where most of our higher-order processing takes place. We will look at this in more detail now.

Cerebral cortex

The cerebral cortex is split down the midline into two halves (called **cerebral hemispheres**) which are connected together by a band of nerve fibres called the **corpus callosum** (Figure 3.6). It is also divided into four regions called the **cerebral lobes**. These are the **frontal lobe**, the **parietal lobe**, the **temporal lobe** and the **occipital lobe** (Figure 3.7). Hence, all four lobes have a left and right half. Note that for the temporal lobe these are two separate regions whereas for the other three lobes the left and right halves are adjacent and meet in the midline. Each lobe performs certain functions and the major ones will be outlined here.

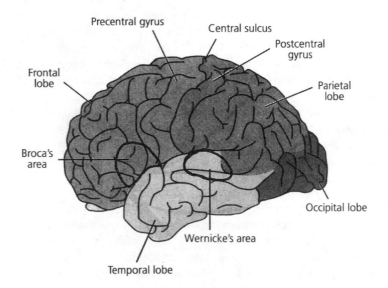

Figure 3.7 **The cerebral cortex**

Frontal lobes

The frontal lobes lie anterior to the **central sulcus** and contain the brain region responsible for initiating voluntary movement. This region is the **motor cortex** (in an area called the precentral gyrus) and is indicated in Figure 3.7. Along its length all regions of our bodies are represented with their own specialised area. However, these areas are not in proportion with the actual size of each region, but rather the fineness of motor control that the area possesses. So, for example, our fingers are represented by a bigger area than our backs.

The most rostral (head-end) region of this lobe is called the prefrontal cortex and plays a role in some aspects of problem-solving and in the facial expression of emotion. Indeed, a prefrontal **lobotomy** (severing the prefrontal cortex from the rest of the brain) used to be performed to reduce anti-social behaviour in severe schizophrenics who did not respond to drug treatment, although it is now believed that this operation has very little value. The prefrontal cortex is also critically involved in working memory (Freedman and Oscar-Berman 1986) and in planning (or 'intending') a motor action. Also located in the frontal lobe, but only on the left side, is an area called **Broca's area** (Figure 3.7). This region is responsible for speech output and will be discused more fully later.

Parietal lobes

The parietal lobes lie posterior to the central sulcus and are specialised for interpreting information from our bodies, for example, touch information. The **somatosensory cortex** lies posterior to the central sulcus in the postcentral gyrus (Figure 3.7). Like the motor cortex, this region also has an area for each region of our bodies and its proportions are in relation to our sensitivity rather than to actual body area. So, for example, our lips are represented by an area roughly the same size as our entire torso.

From a psychological viewpoint, the parietal lobes contain part of the association cortex, a term used simply to refer to the part of the cortex where much of the integration of information from different **modalities** takes place.

Temporal lobes

The temporal lobes are, perhaps, the most interesting from a psychological perspective. Using, largely, neuropsychological evidence, it has been shown that they contain the major part of the association cortex and are involved in a diverse range of psychological functions. These include memory (Scoville and Milner 1957), emotional behaviour (Schroder *et al.* 1995), face perception (Sergent and Signoret 1992), auditory perception (Auerbach *et al.* 1982) and speech comprehension (Auerbach *et al.* 1982). The last of these takes place in a region called **Wernicke's area** (Figure 3.7) which, like Broca's area in the frontal lobe, is only found on the left side. We will look at some of these later in the chapter.

Occipital lobe

The occipital lobe is situated at the back of the brain. The lobe is devoted almost entirely to visual processing. This indicates how important the visual sense is. We owe much of our understanding of how this region works to two researchers called Hubel and Weisel. The lobe is divided into a primary visual area (also called the striate cortex) and secondary areas (called the peristriate cortex). The primary visual area allows us to form an internal image of what we see and the secondary areas begin the interpretation of this image.

These descriptions of the lobes of the cerebral cortex might make it appear that they have different functions and work independently of each other. You should remember that these divisions are nothing more than anatomical conveniences that allow us to clearly define which area of the cortex we are referring to. As far as the brain is concerned, the entire cortex works as an integrated information processing unit.

Functions of the CNS

The intention here is not to provide a detailed analysis of CNS functioning but rather to give you a flavour of how CNS activity affects behaviour. Three areas have been chosen: arousal, for which there is a major role for hindbrain and midbrain structures; emotion, for which subcortical forebrain structures are important; and language, for which the cerebral cortex is vital.

Arousal

An important area for arousing the brain to make it alert to incoming stimuli is the reticular formation. This is a network of neurons in and around the hindbrain and extending up through the midbrain. The role of these neurons in alerting the cortex has been shown by studies that alter an animal's responsiveness to external stimuli. For example, Fuster (1958) trained monkeys to discriminate between two objects. He then decreased the exposure time to these objects so that the animals could no longer discriminate between them. If he then stimulated the reticular formation whilst presenting the stimuli he found that the animals could discriminate at very short exposure times. It seems that the stimulation aroused the brain so that it was now more alert to the external environment.

Emotion

Many of the elements of emotion are controlled by a subcortical region of the brain called the limbic system. This system comprises a number of structures including the hypothalamus, the amygdala, the septum, the hippocampus, the mammillary bodies and the cingulate cortex. Papez (1937) suggested that a circuit within this system (the Papez circuit) was involved in both the feelings of emotion and in emotional expression. He believed that the circuit for feelings involved the hypothalamus, mammillary bodies and cingulate cortex and that the circuit for expression centred around the hypothalamus. Revisions to this early idea have added the amygdala and hippocampus and downplayed the cortex but it is, nevertheless, true that the limbic system controls much of our emotional behaviour. The series book on motivation, emotion and stress covers this topic in greater detail.

Language

There are two major cortical regions that are important for the normal use of language. Both of these are marked on Figure 3.7. The first lies in the cortex of the frontal lobe and is called Broca's area. This is named after Paul Broca who discovered that when this region of the brain is damaged then the patient has difficulty in producing normal speech. However, such a patient can usually understand what is being said. This suggests that Broca's area is important for speech production but not for speech comprehension.

Another speech area lies in the cortex of the temporal lobe and is called Wernicke's area (Figure 3.7) after Carl Wernicke. He discovered that patients with lesions in this region were unable to comprehend what was being said. They appeared to speak normally in some ways (using nouns, verbs, adjectives, etc.) but what they said didn't make any sense. It seems that this area of the brain is responsible for the proper comprehension of speech.

One should note that in most people these two language areas lie only in the cortex on the left side of the brain. These features of language and its lateralisation are described in detail in the series book on cortical functions.

Chapter summary

We have seen how it is useful to divide the nervous system into two main sections: the CNS and the PNS. The CNS consists of the brain and spinal cord, while the PNS is divided into the somatic and autonomic nervous systems. We have also reviewed the structure of the brain and the terms used to describe the relative positions of its components. The hindbrain, midbrain and forebrain regions all have a number of structures within them and we have considered the major ones in each region. Only a brief indication of functions has been given here. In Chapter 6 we consider in detail the brain regions associated with homeostasis. Other books in this series give more detailed accounts of the role of the CNS in a variety of behaviours, including sleep, motivation and emotion, language, vision, and so on.

How many boxes can you fill in below concerning the organisation of the nervous system? Some of them have been filled in for you.

When you have finished go back over the text and see whether or not you were correct. Fill in any boxes you missed and correct those that you got wrong.

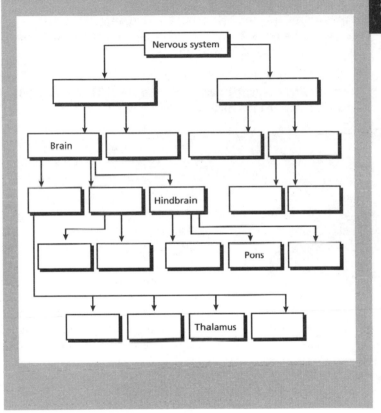

Further reading

Kalat, J.W. (1998) *Biological Psychology*. 6th edn Brooks/Cole Publishing Company, Belmont, CA. ISBN 0–534–34893–9. An excellent all-round text which deals with this particular section in a lot of detail in Chapter 4.

There is an associated internet study centre at:
http://psychstudy.brookscole.com/kalat_bio.shtml.
You will need a user-id and password to gain entry to the study centre but this can be obtained by your tutor.

Pinel, J.P.J. (1998) *A Colorful Introduction to the Anatomy of the Human Brain*. Allyn & Bacon, Boston, MA. This is an excellent book describing the structure of the brain.

The autonomic nervous system

Introduction

The autonomic nervous system (ANS) is a branch of the nervous system which is concerned with regulating the internal state of the organism. The main reason for considering it within a psychology text is because it plays an important role in the control of emotional behaviours. For example, it has a major role in the **'fight or flight'** response that occurs when we are faced with a dangerous situation.

Structure of the ANS

Sympathetic and parasympathetic branches

The ANS serves many of the internal organs of our body. It is composed of two subsystems, the **sympathetic nervous system** and the **parasympathetic nervous system**. These two branches work in a complementary way to regulate the balance of the internal environment. For example, activity in the sympathetic nervous system serves to increase the heart rate, whereas activity in the parasympathetic nervous system serves to reduce the heart rate. Table 4.1 shows some of the organs affected by the ANS and the respective actions of the two branches. Note that not all organs are innervated by both branches of the ANS. For example, the **adrenal glands** are only innervated by the sympathetic nervous system. First we need to consider briefly the anatomy of the ANS and then look at the brain areas that control it.

Anatomy of the ANS

Both branches of the ANS send out efferent neurons which travel from the brain along the spinal cord. At various points along the spinal cord fibres branch off to innervate the organs listed in Table 4.1. However, the two systems differ in their structure after the fibres leave the spinal cord. For the sympathetic nervous system, groups of fibres travel only a short way from the spinal cord and then make

Table 4.1 Actions of the ANS		
ORGAN	SYMPATHETIC ACTION	PARASYMPATHETIC ACTION
Eye	Dilates pupils	Constricts pupils
Mouth	Inhibits salivation	Stimulates salivation
Lungs	Relaxes airways	Constricts airways
Heart	Increases heart rate	Decreases heart rate
Sweat glands	Increases sweating	NO ACTION
Intestines	NO ACTION	Dilates blood vessels
Stomach	Inhibits digestion	Stimulates digestion
Liver	Stimulates glucose release	NO ACTION
Adrenal glands	Stimulates adrenaline release	NO ACTION
Skin	Constricts blood vessels	Dilates blood vessels
Bladder	Relaxes bladder	Contracts bladder
Penis	Stimulates ejaculation	Stimulates erection

synaptic connections with **ganglia**. (A ganglion is a collection of cell bodies of neurons densely packed into a small area.) The ganglia then send out other efferent neurons to innervate the various organs in that region. For example, the **celiac ganglion** sends efferent neurons to the stomach, liver, kidney, adrenal glands, sweat glands and skin.

For the parasympathetic nervous system, the structure is similar except that the ganglia lie very close to the end organ. Hence the ganglia tend to only provide efferent neurons that innervate one end organ (e.g. the kidney). Figure 4.1 shows these differences in schematic form.

Central control of the ANS

The ANS is controlled by structures in the brainstem, and also the hypothalamus, a structure in the diencephalon, that we met in Chapter 3 (and discuss more fully in Chapter 5). Hess (1954) discovered that there were two parts of the hypothalamus that seemed to exert control over the ANS: the **posterior nucleus** which controls the sympathetic branch and the **anterior nucleus** controls the parasympathetic branch. Hess (1954) showed that this was the case by electrically stimulating these structures. When he stimulated the posterior nucleus he found responses that were consistent with sympathetic activity (increased heart rate and sweating, etc.). When he stimulated the ante-

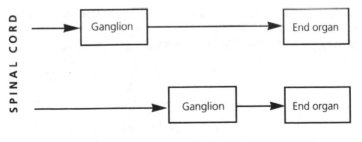

Figure 4.1 **Schematic showing ganglion placement for the two branches of the ANS**

rior nucleus he found that heart rate slowed and there was a general calming of internal and external behaviour, a result consistent with parasympathetic activity.

It is not surprising that the brainstem region exerts control over the ANS as the brainstem contains many structures that regulate vital functions such as respiration, circulation, feeding, thirst, body temperature, etc. However, it is not entirely clear whether these structures play a more important role in stimulating ANS activity or in causing the release of controlling hormones. What is clear is that such regulation of vital functions is achieved by a combination of ANS activity and endocrine (hormonal) activity. We will examine this in the next two chapters but for now we will concentrate on the functions of the ANS.

Progress exercise

Make a large diagram of the body. Mark on it all the parts that are innervated by the ANS. Indicate on the diagram what the effect of sympathetic nervous system activity is on each body part. Do the same for the parasympathetic nervous system.

Functions of the ANS

In this section we will examine the role of the ANS in two differing scenarios. The first is how the ANS contributes to the formation of ulcers. The second is the role of the ANS in the 'fight or flight' situation.

'Executive stress' and the formation of ulcers

Most people are familiar with the view that high-powered executives are more likely to develop stomach ulcers due to the stresses of their job. A study that tried to address this was conducted by Brady *et al.* (1958). In this experiment two monkeys were put in chairs. Both monkeys had one foot attached to an electrode that could deliver an electric shock. One of the monkeys (the passive monkey) had no way of avoiding the shock but the other monkey (the executive monkey) could press a lever to prevent a shock being delivered. If the executive monkey pressed the lever then both monkeys were spared a shock on that trial. If the monkey failed to press the lever in time then both monkeys received a shock. In this way the executive monkey was in total control of shock avoidance.

Brady *et al.* found that the executive monkey developed ulcers whereas the passive monkey did not. They had predicted this because they claimed that the executive monkey was under greater stress due to having the responsibility not just for its own shock but also for the other monkey's shock. However, this conclusion may be an oversimplification, and a number of criticisms of the experiment suggest why.

In the study the monkeys used as executives were all proven good learners and so they mastered the association between pressing the lever and preventing the shock in just a few hours or less. Once learned, neither monkey then ever received a shock. One might argue, therefore, that the only difference between the monkeys was the high level of physical exertion endured by the executive monkey. Perhaps this caused the ulcers.

In another experiment by Foltz and Millett (1964) the executive monkey experiment was repeated but this time a new, naive executive was introduced every few weeks. It was noticed that when a new executive was brought in it took a few hours for it to learn the task and during this time the passive monkey would become highly agitated. In this scenario it was the passive monkey that developed stomach ulcers. Foltz and Millett suggested that the passive monkeys developed ulcers because of the high arousal levels associated with the unavoidable shock.

So how might we explain the association between stress and the development of stomach ulcers? Recent evidence suggests that it is not what happens during the stressful period that causes ulcer formation but what happens during the period immediately afterwards. During the stressful period levels of sympathetic nervous system activity are high. After the stress is over the parasympathetic nervous system rebounds with a high level of activity. One of the functions of the parasympathetic nervous system is to cause a release of digestive juices. If there is nothing in the stomach to be digested then the digestive juices will damage the walls of the stomach and intestines and cause ulcers. It would seem, therefore, that one good thing to do after a stressful situation has passed is to eat so that the digestive juices will be used up.

Fight or flight

Imagine that you are a little mouse and you spot a cat in the near distance. Imagine also that it has spotted you and starts to give chase. You have two choices. You can either stand and try to defend yourself or you can run like crazy. If you are a sensible mouse you will choose the latter but either way your sympathetic nervous system will be called into action. Look at Table 4.1 again and remind yourself of the outcomes of sympathetic activity. We can take each one in turn and analyse whether or not it is a useful function to aid running away.

- The pupils dilate. This allows plenty of light to enter the eye so that the animal can see where it is going.
- The mouth dries out. The last thing you need to worry about is anything to do with digesting your food. If you don't survive it will hardly matter. Hence you must make all sources of energy available for fleeing.
- The airways are relaxed. This helps you to breath more easily so that you can get more oxygen into the blood. When you are doing a strenuous activity (like running) your muscles will use up oxygen more quickly.
- Heart rate increases. Again, this enables blood to be pumped around the body more quickly to speed up the supply of oxygen to where it is needed.
- Increased sweating. The increase in activity will increase the heat that the body is generating. To counter this sweating deposits fluid onto the skin's surface where it will evaporate and cool the body down.
- Digestion by the stomach ceases. As with salivating, the last place you need to expend energy at a time like this is in digesting food.
- **Glucose** release from the liver is stimulated. Once again this is about energy. As glucose is the major source of energy for cells there needs to be a plentiful supply in the blood. That which has previously been stored in the liver is now released.

- **Adrenaline** is released from the **adrenal medulla**. This is a hormone that is released into the blood where it has a general mobilising effect.
- Blood vessels to the skin constrict. If any injury is sustained whilst fleeing the lowered blood supply to the skin will prevent excessive bleeding.
- The bladder relaxes. The bladder is a muscle that is usually contracted until you wish to urinate. The energy for this is more useful elsewhere and so the bladder relaxes and urination takes place.
- Ejaculation. Obviously, the sympathetic nervous system's control over ejaculation is not of functional value at this time.

We can see that all except one of the actions of the sympathetic nervous system help the animal to spring into action. If the scenario called for standing and fighting (e.g. during a territorial battle) then these same considerations would hold true. For this reason, whether fighting or fleeing, the body shuts down unwanted processes and mobilises oxygen and energy to where it might be needed.

Chapter summary

In this chapter we have seen that the ANS is divided into two branches, the sympathetic nervous system and the parasympathetic nervous system. Between them they regulate the internal body state so that it can meet the immediate needs as determined by the external environment. The ANS plays a role in the consequences of excessively stressful situations (e.g. 'executive stress'). It is the parasympathetic nervous system that is probably responsible for the development of stomach ulcers under these conditions. The sympathetic nervous system is particularly important in the 'fight or flight' situation in which the heart, lungs, blood supply and energy systems must be mobilised in readiness for fighting or running away.

Review exercise

Imagine you are in a fight or flight situation. For each of the organs listed below state the action of the sympathetic nervous system and briefly describe what the benefits of this action are under these circumstances.

Heart

Lungs

Eyes

Adrenal glands

Stomach

Liver

Skin

Sweat glands

Further reading

Kalat, J.W. (1998) *Biological Psychology*. 6th edn. Brooks/Cole Publishing Company, Belmont, CA. ISBN 0–534–34893–9. An excellent all-round text which deals with this particular section in a lot of detail.

There is an associated internet study centre at:
http://psychstudy.brookscole.com/kalat_bio.shtml
You will need a user-id and password to gain entry to the study centre but this can be obtained by your tutor.

The endocrine system

Introduction

We have seen how the ANS reacts to the needs of the body with a speedy response. There is also a much slower response to external events that is carried via messengers in the blood. The system that controls these responses is the **endocrine system** and the messengers are called **hormones**. The endocrine system is similar to the nervous system in some ways. Just as neurons carry particular neurotransmitter substances that only work at certain receptor sites, so the endocrine system releases hormones that, too, only work at specific receptor sites around the body.

The endocrine system has a two-tiered system of hormones. **Glands** are defined by the fact that they release hormones into the bloodstream. The hormones then have an effect at a variety of body locations. The glands are controlled by brain sites that release their own hormones (called **releasing hormones**). These releasing hormones tell the glands to release more of their hormones. You can see, therefore, that this complicated process is quite slow.

As well as reacting to external events, the endocrine system controls a number of internal body processes. In this chapter we will look at endocrine reactions to stress, as an example of a response to external events, and the endocrine control over the menstrual cycle, as an example of the regulation of internal body processes. In the next chapter we will see the role of the endocrine system in homeostasis, where both external and internal influences must be monitored and regulated.

Hormone release by the endocrine system

The hypothalamus and pituitary gland

I have already suggested in the introduction that the endocrine system regulates the distribution of hormones around the body and that there are a number of different elements to the system. Figure 5.1 shows a schematic representation of these elements. There are two brain sites that regulate the release of hormones. These are the hypothalamus and the pituitary gland.

The hypothalamus is part of the diencephalon and has a number of different nuclei with differing functions. Some of these nuclei are involved in the regulation of endocrine function. The hypothalamus regulates the secretions of the pituitary gland which is itself made up of two discrete areas, the **posterior pituitary** and the **anterior pituitary**. Control over the posterior pituitary is neuronal. Two nuclei in the hypothalamus (the **paraventricular nucleus** and the **supraoptic nucleus**) send axons to the posterior pituitary gland. However, instead of releasing neurotransmitter substances these neurons secrete hormones directly into the blood **capillaries** of the posterior pituitary. Hence the control of the posterior pituitary by the hypothalamus is **neurohormonal**. For the anterior pituitary the story is different. Here neurons in the hypothalamus (more distributed than for the posterior pituitary) secrete a number of releasing hormones into the local blood supply. The blood then travels the short distance to the anterior pituitary gland where the releasing hormones activate cells in the anterior pituitary to release their hormones into the blood. Hence this control from the hypothalamus is truly hormonal.

Perhaps the most important part of the endocrine system is the pituitary gland (sometimes referred to as the master gland). As well as being a true gland in its own right, part of the pituitary gland serves to cause other glands around the body to release their hormones. The pituitary gland sticks out from the base of the brain just below the hypothalamus and is joined to the hypothalamus by the **pituitary**

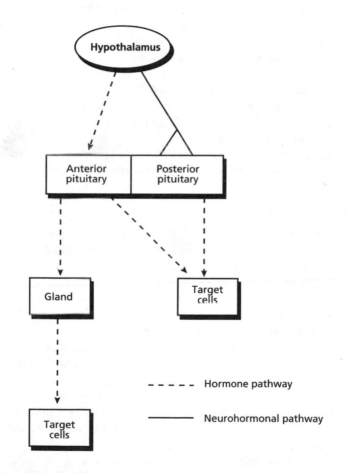

Figure 5.1 **A schematic representation of the elements of the endocrine system**

stalk. As already mentioned, the pituitary gland is divided into two parts, the anterior pituitary and the posterior pituitary. In the posterior pituitary hormones are secreted into the blood which then act directly on their target organs, whereas the anterior pituitary (with two exceptions) secretes hormones into the blood which stimulate other glands to secrete their hormones.

The hormones released by the posterior pituitary gland travel via the blood to their target cells. However, most of the hormones from the anterior pituitary gland are **stimulating hormones** which travel to other glands. Here they cause further hormones to be released. If we review the process so far we can see that hormone release via the anterior pituitary path follows the sequence:

1   activity of the hypothalamus causes the release of a releasing hormone which
2   leads to the release of a stimulating hormone from the pituitary gland which
3   circulates in the blood until it reaches an end organ where
4   it causes the release of another hormone into the blood.

Glandular hormones

Table 5.1 shows a selection of the various hormones released by the endocrine system. The posterior pituitary gland releases two hormones into the bloodstream. One of these is **oxytocin**, which causes contraction of the uterus and also stimulates the mammary glands to secrete milk. The other is **arginine vasopressin (AVP)**, which stimulates the kidneys to reabsorb water from the urine. AVP is also known as **antidiuretic hormone (ADH)**.

The hypothalamus secretes a number of releasing hormones which activate the anterior pituitary gland. **Thyrotropin-releasing hormone (TRH)** stimulates the anterior pituitary to release **thyroid-stimulating hormone (TSH)** into the bloodstream. This then stimulates the thyroid gland (which is made up of two glands on either side of the larynx) to release **thyroxine**. Thyroxine stimulates metabolism in cells and also plays a role in promoting growth.

Corticotrophin-releasing hormone (CRH) causes the anterior pituitary to release **adrenocorticotrophic hormone (ACTH)**. This then acts on the adrenal cortex which is the outer part of the adrenal gland.

There is an adrenal gland situated just above each kidney. The adrenal cortex secretes two different types of **adrenocorticoid** hormones. **Mineralocorticoids** such as **aldosterone** regulate the level of salts such as sodium and potassium in the body. They do this by allowing or preventing the kidney from secreting salts into the urine. **Glucocorticoids** such as **cortisol** promote the conversion of proteins and fats to carbohydrates which are a useable source of energy for the body.

Gonadotrophin-releasing hormone (GnRH) stimulates the release of two different sex hormones from the anterior pituitary. One of these is **follicle-stimulating hormone (FSH)**. In males this hormone causes the testes to release **testosterone**. This promotes the development and maintenance of male sexual characteristics (voice-breaking, facial hair, etc.). In females, FSH causes the ovaries to release **oestrogen** which promotes the development and maintenance of female secondary sexual characteristics (breast development, female distri- bution of body hair and fat, etc.). The other pituitary sex hormone is **luteinising hormone**. In males this, too, causes the testes to secrete testosterone. However, in females, once an ovum has been released from the ovary, it causes the follicle in which the ovum has matured to secrete **progesterone**. The progesterone then readies the wall of the womb for pregnancy in the event that fertilisation should occur.

The hypothalamus also secretes two opposing hormones that regu- late growth. **Somatocrinin** causes the anterior pituitary to secrete **growth hormone** whereas **somatostatin** causes the anterior pituitary to stop secreting growth hormone.

Finally, the act of a baby sucking on a mother's nipple causes the anterior pituitary to release **prolactin** which promotes the secretion of milk. The hypothalamus regulates the termination of this by secreting **prolactin-inhibiting factor (PIF)**.

There is one further gland shown in Table 5.1 that is not controlled by the hypothalamus or pituitary gland. This is the pancreas. The pancreas secretes two hormones, **insulin** and **glucagon**, as a direct response to the level of glucose in the blood. Insulin drives glucose into cells where it can be utilised for energy or, in the case of the liver, stored as a substance called **glycogen**. Glucagon does the reverse, preventing glucose entering cells and promoting the conversion of glycogen in the liver back into glucose.

Table 5.1 Table of selected endocrine hormones and their actions

Hypothalamic hormone	Pituitary hormone	Gland	Glandular hormone	Target	Action
Thyrotropin-releasing hormone (TRH)	Thyroid-stimulating hormone (TSH)	Thyroid gland	Thyroxine	Non-specific	Stimulates metabolism
Gonadotrophin-releasing hormone (GnRH)	Follicle-stimulating hormone (FSH)	Testes	Testosterone	Non-specific	Stimulates development and maintenance of male sexual characteristics
		Ovaries	Oestrogen	Non-specific	Stimulates development and maintenance of female secondary sexual characteristics
	Luteinising hormone	Testes	Testosterone	Non-specific	Stimulates development and maintenance of male sexual characteristics
		Ovaries	Progesterone		Stimulates development and maintenance of female secondary sexual characteristics

Corticotrophin-releasing hormone (CRH)	Adrenocorticotrophic hormone (ACTH)	Adrenal cortex	Glucocorticoids	Non-specific	Stimulates storage of glycogen and helps maintain blood sugar levels
			Mineralocorticoids	Non-specific	Regulates sodium and potassium metabolism
Somatocrinin (excites) and somatostatin (inhibits)	Growth hormone			Non-specific	Stimulates growth
Prolactin-inhibiting factor (PIF)	Prolactin	Mammary glands			Stimulates milk secretion
	Oxytocin	Mammary glands			Stimulates uterine contraction and milk secretion
	Arginine vasopressin (AVP) – a.k.a. antidiuretic hormone (ADH)			Kidneys	Stimulates increased water reabsorption
		Pancreas	Insulin	Liver	Stores blood glucose as glycogen
			Glucagon	Liver	Converts glycogen to glucose which is released into the blood

Feedback mechanisms

The complexity of the endocrine system, with its hypothalamic, pituitary and glandular hormones, allows for a great degree of control over internal bodily functions. This is best illustrated if we consider some of the **feedback mechanisms** that the system uses. Figure 5.2 shows the regulation of the adrenocorticoids. As already described, the hypothalamus secretes CRH which causes the anterior pituitary to secrete ACTH into the bloodstream. This, in turn, causes the **adrenal cortex** to release adrenocorticoids into the blood. The level of adrenocorticoids in the blood is monitored by cells in both the pituitary and hypothalamus. If too much adrenocorticoid is present in the blood then release by the pituitary and hypothalamus is inhibited. Why the inhibition at both sites? Well, imagine that information coming from the external environment causes brain regions to excite the hypothalamus. If inhibition occurred only at the pituitary then the level of inhibition might not be sufficient to override the release of CRH by the hypothalamus due to its excitation. Inhibiting the hypothalamus directly decreases the amount of CRH released and this

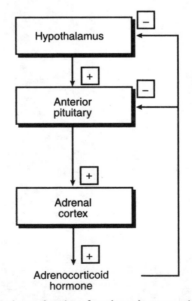

Figure 5.2 **Feedback mechanism for the adrenocorticoids**

enables the inhibition at the pituitary to properly regulate the release of adrenocorticoids from the adrenal cortex.

Not all regulation is this complicated. In the pancreas, too little glucose in the blood inhibits the insulin cells from releasing insulin and stimulates the glucagon cells to release glucagon which then causes the liver to release glucose into the blood. Too high a level of blood glucose simply has the reverse effect. However, the level of blood glucose can become dangerously high or dangerously low as in forms of diabetes.

Summary

As you can see from the above discussion, the endocrine system performs a great many different functions that are regulated in order to meet the internal needs of the organism. In this respect the functions are similar to those of the ANS. In the last section of this chapter we will look at two particular functions of the endocrine system in a little more detail.

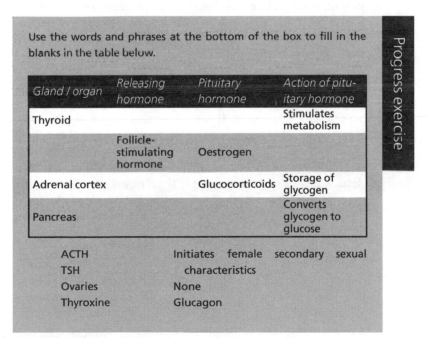

Use the words and phrases at the bottom of the box to fill in the blanks in the table below.

Progress exercise

Gland / organ	Releasing hormone	Pituitary hormone	Action of pituitary hormone
Thyroid			Stimulates metabolism
	Follicle-stimulating hormone	Oestrogen	
Adrenal cortex		Glucocorticoids	Storage of glycogen
Pancreas			Converts glycogen to glucose

ACTH	Initiates female secondary sexual
TSH	characteristics
Ovaries	None
Thyroxine	Glucagon

Functions of the endocrine system

Endocrine reactions to stress

In the last chapter we looked at the way in which the ANS reacts to a 'fight or flight' situation. Such a situation is stressful but it is usually temporary and so the endocrine system, with its slow response times, hardly gets involved. However, we live in an environment where we are less likely to resolve a situation as quickly as we are biologically designed to do. For example, running away or fighting your tutor is not going to resolve the stress you might feel as an examination approaches. Such **stress** is referred to as chronic stress and it persists long enough for the endocrine system to play a very important part.

Under conditions of short-term stress the hypothalamus causes the anterior pituitary to release ACTH. This travels to the adrenal cortex where it stimulates the release of the glucocorticoids such as cortisol. The released cortisol has beneficial effects as it increases the metabolic rate and elevates the level of glucose in the blood. These are useful events if there is to be a sustained period of physical activity.

Very often we get ourselves into a position where we are suffering long-term stress and often it is in situations where bursts of activity are inappropriate. Under these conditions our natural endocrine responses can be detrimental to our health. The constant release of ACTH leads to prolonged elevated levels of cortisol. This has a number of consequences. Firstly, high levels of cortisol are linked with depression, a state of mind that often accompanies long term stress. Secondly, under normal circumstances receptors in the hypothalamus detect when there are elevated cortisol levels and switch off the release of ACTH (negative feedback). However, high levels of blood cortisol appears to be toxic to the very receptors that detect that the level is high. The consequence is that the high level of cortisol becomes less and less well detected and so the release of ACTH is maintained at a high rate. The third, and probably the most damaging, consequence of prolonged high levels of blood cortisol is the damage done to the immune system. Cortisol is a powerful anti-inflammatory agent and so it prevents the inflammation which surrounds a damaged area from growing too large. An increase in cortisol activity during stress will reduce the normal inflammatory response and thereby suppress the effect of the immune system should it be called into action. Cortisol also has other damaging effects on the immune system which involve the action of white blood cells. These are the cells responsible for killing off foreign bodies such as bacteria, dead cells, virus particles, debris and inorganic matter.

Endocrine control of the menstrual cycle

The menstrual cycle is a periodic variation in hormones and fertility. In humans the period is approximately 28 days. During the month there is a variation in the amounts of circulating sex hormones and this regulates the timing of **ovulation** and **menstruation**. At the beginning of the cycle FSH promotes the growth of follicles within the ovary. From around day 8 the follicles start to produce an oestrogen called estradiol. This causes a sudden surge (around day 10) of luteinising hormone from the anterior pituitary. There is also an increase in FSH release at this time. Together, these hormone surges cause one of the follicles to release an ovum (day 14).

Once the ovum has been released, the follicle, which is now referred to as a **corpus luteum** (yellow body), releases progesterone. The progesterone prepares the uterus wall for the implantation of the ovum should it become fertilised and also inhibits any further release of luteinising hormone from the pituitary gland. The progesterone level is at its peak around day 23 and after that the level rapidly tapers off. By day 28 the prepared uterus wall is shed (menstruation) if no fertilised ovum has been implanted. The cycle then begins again.

The above description illustrates how the endocrine system regulates an internal body process. Note how the rise in the level of progesterone inhibits the further release of luteinising hormone. This is an example of **negative feedback**.

Other aspects of sexual behaviour

There are many aspects of sexual behaviour that are under the control of endocrine functions. The sex hormones (especially androgens) play a critical role in determining whether or not a developing foetus will appear male or female. That is, a genetic male will not develop male genitalia if he is insensitive to **androgens** during development. Hormones are also believed to be involved in the development of sexuality in humans. It is possible that male homosexuality is contributed to by a lowered level of testosterone during brain development (Ellis and Ames 1987). Finally, hormones are also important for the control of maternal and paternal behaviour. A contemporary piece of research concerning the role of hormones in monogamy and polygamy in different species of vole is included as a key research article in Chapter 10.

Chapter summary

In this chapter we have looked at the endocrine system and the types of function that it controls. This system is controlled by the hypothalamus and the pituitary gland by one of two mechanisms, a neuronal one (posterior pituitary) or a neurohormonal one (anterior pituitary). Another important part of endocrine control is feedback. This allows for the correct amounts of a hormone to be present in the bloodstream as and when required. In Chapter 6 we will see how ANS and endocrine control work in tandem to regulate some behavioural functions.

Further reading

Kalat, J.W. (1998) *Biological Psychology*. 6th edn. Brooks/Cole Publishing Company, Belmont, CA. ISBN 0–534–34893–9. An excellent all-round text which has a chapter on hormones that is very easy to read.

There is an associated internet study centre at:
http://psychstudy.brookscole.com/kalat_bio.shtml
You will need a user-id and password to gain entry to the study centre but this can be obtained by your tutor.

Below is a sketch of the some of the major endocrine glands in their correct places in the body. Label each gland and give a brief description of its function.

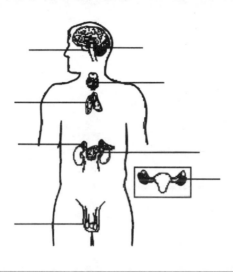

Homeostasis

Introduction

In this chapter we consider **homeostasis** as an example of how the CNS, ANS and endocrine system work together. The term homeostasis refers to the maintenance of a relatively stable state within our bodies. In the first part of the chapter we take a closer look at exactly what this means. The rest of the chapter details three major homeostatic mechanisms, namely, the regulation of our nutritional content (eating), the regulation of our water content (drinking), and the regulation of our body heat (temperature regulation). As you work through the chapter you will see that all three mechanisms are kept in balance by a combination of hormonal and ANS activity, all of which is coordinated by central brain processes.

What is homeostasis?

As I am writing this book in World Cup year I will start, if I may, with a football analogy. Imagine that you want to have a game of football. If the ball is not pumped up enough then it will not bounce properly. If it is blown up too much then it will burst. Indeed, professional footballers will tell you that small diversions from the correct pressure make it difficult to play properly. There is, therefore, a limited range of pressures over which the football can function as a football. The same is true of the constituents of our bodies. For example, many of the chemical reactions in our body are helped by the presence of enzymes. Enzymes will only work within a limited temperature range. Therefore, the body must maintain its temperature within certain limits. The mechanisms for this and all of the other balances are called homeostatic mechanisms.

There are a number of features of homeostasis that are worth pointing out before we look at the details.

- The ideal range for any component is called the **set point**. It is called a point rather than a range because for many components the range is so limited that it is virtually a point.
- Each component has to have a **detector** to monitor whether the set point is being maintained.
- There must be a **correctional mechanism** to make alterations when the detector registers a significant deviation from the set point.
- The detector and its correctional mechanism represent the reactive process of homeostasis. That is to say, these features allow our bodies to react to changes in the set point when they occur. There is also, however, a prospective process of homeostasis. Most animals are able to anticipate future changes that are likely to occur. We must, therefore, also look at the behaviours that an animal indulges in to avoid the need for such reactive processes. For example, if we were about to take a walk on a hot summer's day we might have a drink before we set off in anticipation of (and as a prevention against) a future need for drinking.

Bearing these features in mind, we can now look at three specific homeostatic mechanisms. We will start with temperature regulation as this represents one of the simpler mechanisms.

Temperature regulation

When you think you have a fever you measure your temperature using a thermometer which you usually place under your tongue. Why there? Why not rest the thermometer on your skin? The reason is that you are trying to estimate your **core body temperature**, which is the temperature of your internal organs. By measuring an area rich in a blood supply that is close to the surface of the tongue you are quite accurately measuring blood temperature as an indication of core body temperature.

It is the core body temperature that we try to maintain at the set point (approximately 37° C in humans). We do this using a combination of temperature receptors in the brain and responses by the ANS.

Control mechanisms of temperature regulation

One of the most important temperature monitors lies in an area of the hypothalamus called the **preoptic area**. This area very simply monitors its own temperature (Nelson and Prosser 1981). If the preoptic area gets too cold it initiates **vasoconstriction** of the blood vessels in the skin via the sympathetic nervous system. This prevents a lot of warm blood from being sent to the skin where it would be cooled by the air. There is also erection of the hairs on the skin (commonly referred to as goosebumps but properly called **piloerection**). This traps a thin layer of air next to the skin which acts as insulation (in much the same way as a duvet cover works). In fact, goosebumps do little for humans as their hairs are so short but in other animals, with thick fur, this is a good way of conserving heat. A third response is to shiver. This is caused by a rhythmic contraction of the muscles near the skin's surface. These three mechanisms serve to keep heat from being lost through the skin and so keep our insides warm.

If the preoptic area becomes too hot the blood vessels of the skin dilate to lead more blood there so that heat can be lost through the skin. The sweat glands are activated via the sympathetic nervous system. By moistening the skin, sweat acts to cool the skin and thereby helps to cool the insides.

Behavioural changes in anticipation of temperature requirements

As well as physiological mechanisms, there are a number of behaviours which prevent excessive heat loss or heat gain. Several animals huddle together in the cold and rotate their position so as to take turns in being exposed to the cold of the outside. To prevent heat gain, many animals find a shady spot or bury themselves in the ground. What is important here is that the behaviours are not always simply a response to the prevailing conditions. Animals will behave in certain ways in anticipation of exposure to heat or cold. These behaviours, like the physiological changes, are also partly under the control of the preoptic area. However, there are also regions of the posterior hypothalamus that play a role in these activities.

Eating

The homeostatic regulation of eating is a little different to that of temperature regulation. Whereas the need for warming up or cooling down can be effected pretty much immediately by constricting or dilating the blood vessels to the skin, the need for nutrients cannot be satisfied so quickly. Any shortfall in, say, carbohydrate requirement has to wait until digestion has taken place (which is several hours). This means that the system has to have two mechanisms to maintain a balance. The first is a **hunger mechanism** that can monitor current needs and anticipate future requirements. The second is a **satiety mechanism** that can indicate when enough food has been ingested in the present to satisfy the demands of the near future. We will look at each of these in turn but we must first examine, briefly, the process of metabolism. This will help you to understand the basis upon which hunger and satiety mechanisms work.

Metabolism

Metabolism is the process by which we extract and store fuels from the blood in times of plenty and use our reserves when fuel levels in the blood are low. Our major (but not the only) source of fuel for providing our cells with energy is the carbohydrate called glucose. When there is plenty of glucose in the blood (e.g. as we digest a meal containing carbohydrates), the pancreas secretes a hormone called insulin. The insulin helps glucose to enter the cells of our body. Any excess glucose enters the liver and there it is converted to glycogen and stored. When there is not enough glucose in the blood (some time after a meal), the level of insulin in the blood is low but the pancreas now secretes another hormone called glucagon which converts the stored glycogen back into glucose. So the liver acts as a short-term store for glucose. This store is mainly for the benefit of brain cells rather than other cells. The reason for this is that insulin is not required for getting glucose into brain cells whereas it is required for getting glucose into the other cells. Since blood insulin levels are low when glucagon levels are high, the glucose released can, mostly, only be used by the brain.

You may be wondering what the other cells use when the level of blood glucose is low. Well, there is another energy store in our bodies in the form of fats. Fats are mainly stored, as many of us like myself know, just under the skin of the abdomen. They are stored in the form of **adipose tissue**. When this store is called upon, fat cells convert the stored fat into **glycerol** (which the liver converts to glucose for the brain) and **fatty acids** (which the rest of the body can use directly). Activity in the fat cells is controlled from three sources: direct stimulation via the sympathetic nervous system; glucagon released by the pancreas; and noradrenaline and adrenaline released by the adrenal medulla.

Finally, the period soon after a meal when energy is being stored is called the **absorptive phase** and the period when energy stores are being used up is called the **fasting phase**.

Hunger

There is no simple answer to the question of what makes us hungry. However, there is some good evidence to suggest that it involves the monitoring of levels of blood glucose. Lowered levels of blood glucose inhibit the secretion of insulin and initiate fat cell activity via the sympathetic nervous system. This marks the start of the fasting phase. However, this in itself does not initiate the motivation to feed. We must also have a monitor which tells us that blood glucose levels are getting too low and that replenishment should happen soonish. This is a bit like finding that your car's petrol tank is only one quarter full.

The glucostatic hypothesis

One hypothesis concerning the trigger for hunger is the **glucostatic hypothesis** (Mayer 1952). This suggests that there are cells in the brain (probably in the **lateral hypothalamus**) that are receptors for the level of blood glucose and whose firing rate is linked to the availability of glucose. A change in their firing rate due to low glucose levels is thought to initiate the desire to search for food. There is good evidence to back up the belief that the monitor is in the lateral hypothalamus. Grossman *et al.* (1978) made kainic acid lesions here. These destroyed the cell bodies of the lateral hypothalamus but left intact the fibres that pass through the region but do not make synaptic contact here. They found that feeding behaviour was severely impaired. However, there is also some evidence that contradicts this hypothesis. Blass and Kraly (1974) destroyed the lateral hypothalamus of rats but found that eating behaviour was normal.

There is a problem with Mayer's (1952) original belief that the receptors monitored blood glucose. People with untreated diabetes have constant high levels of blood glucose because of a deficiency in insulin (see the previous chapter for the endocrine function of insulin). According to Mayer's theory, therefore, these people should show no hunger. The reverse is in fact true, with diabetics reporting that they are constantly hungry.

Mayer (1953) revised his theory to explain this anomaly. If it were not blood glucose but cellular glucose that were the indicator, then the theory would now be consistent with the findings for diabetics. The insulin deficiency in diabetes prevents the glucose from being transported into cells (hence keeping the blood level high). More recent evidence (Russek 1971) has suggested that the monitor for cellular glucose is not in any cells but is in the cells of the liver. Russek showed that injections of glucose into food-deprived animals will prevent eating if the glucose is injected into the liver's blood supply but will not prevent eating if it is injected away from this area.

That the liver is the site for the receptors makes sense. The liver is connected to the lateral hypothalamus via the vagus nerve and is also where insulin causes glucose to be converted into glycogen (a type of stored fat). It would appear, then, that the control for eating is dependent on liver glucose levels. However, things are not so simple. If the vagus nerve were the sole carrier of the message to initiate eating then patients who had had a liver transplant (and hence had the vagus nerve severed) would never feel hungry. We must therefore look to see whether there are other mechanisms that might help to uncover more of the picture.

The lipostatic theory

The **lipostatic theory** of hunger suggests that rather than using glucose as a marker for the need to eat, we use body weight to signal hunger. Early evidence for this theory came from Teitelbaum (1955), who showed that lesions to the **ventromedial hypothalamus** in animals resulted in overeating and obesity. The rationale is that the ventromedial hypothalamus monitors body weight and inhibits eating when body weight is at the desired level (the set point). Hence, lesions to the ventromedial hypothalamus reduce this inhibition and the animal continues to eat and eat until a new, higher body weight is sufficient for the inhibition to occur. Hoebel and Teitelbaum (1966) tested this theory by lesioning the ventromedial hypothalamus and allowing the animals to gain weight until it plateaued out at a new obese level. They then forced the animals to eat even more until they became 'superobese'. When they were then allowed to eat freely again their weight dropped back down to its obese level.

It would appear that the marker for body weight is fat. This was discovered by Liebelt *et al.* (1973) when they surgically removed fat from rats that were obese after ventromedial hypothalamic lesions. After fat removal the rats continued to eat until their weight was restored.

To summarise so far, this theory suggests that hunger is controlled by the ventromedial hypothalamus which uses fat as a monitor of body weight. The suggested mechanism is that on reaching the correct body weight, the ventromedial hypothalamus inhibits further eating. However, Han (1967) discovered something that suggested the theory was not wholly accurate. Han found that after ventromedial hypothalamic lesions animals would gain weight even if they did not have access to extra food. To understand why this was happening, we must re-examine the role of the ventromedial hypothalamus.

Under normal circumstances, after a meal we use glucose as a source of energy and store any excess glucose as fat. The pancreas secretes insulin which acts on the liver to achieve this storage. When all the available glucose has been used up the pancreas secretes glucagon to break down the stored fat in the liver. However, the fat is not reconverted into glucose but instead is broken down into free fatty acids. These can be used by the body as an energy source but they are not as energy rich as glucose. In addition, the liver appears to monitor its own energy usage. As glucose is a richer source of energy the cells in the liver can detect the change from glucose use to free fatty acid use and this stimulates the desire to eat.

It would appear that rather than inhibiting the act of eating, the ventromedial hypothalamus inhibits the release of insulin by the pancreas. So if we lesion the ventromedial hypothalamus then the insulin level remains high and the body continues to try to store glucose as glycogen rather than breaking down the glycogen to be used as energy. The consequence is that the liver detects a lower level of available energy and so triggers the desire to eat.

The ischymetric hypothesis

Whilst the glucostatic and lipostatic theories of hunger represent the most popular theories they are by no means the only ones. Another hypothesis, the **ischymetric hypothesis**, suggests that feeding can be regulated by our metabolic rate. When we are in the absorptive phase of metabolism our metabolic rate is higher than when we are in the fasting phase. Nicolaïdis (1987) has suggested that there may be neurons somewhere in the brain that change their rate of firing with changes in their own metabolic rate. As their metabolic rate falls the change in firing rate signals to other neurons that feeding is needed.

To summarise, the initiation of hunger is most likely triggered by both low levels of glucose in the blood and cells, and low levels of free fatty acids. The liver and various brain sites (e.g. the lateral hypothalamus and the ventromedial hypothalamus) detect whether the levels are getting too low. It is unlikely that detection at any single site is sufficient to initiate feeding but the messages from a combination of sites will build up until the motivation to feed is overwhelming.

Satiety

As mentioned at the beginning of the section on eating, there is a time lag between the act of eating and the nutrients being available to cells for metabolism. Why, then, do we not just continue to eat and eat? We don't because along with mechanisms that trigger eating there are mechanisms that trigger the cessation of eating. It is to these satiety mechanisms that we now turn. Detectors for food intake exist both inside and outside the brain. We have already examined the role of the ventromedial hypothalamus and the lateral hypothalamus. Here we will look at four places outside of the brain which provide information to stop eating.

Sight, smell and taste

Information about the smell, look and taste of food all influence the amount of a particular food that we will eat. We learn to associate certain types of food with a high calorie intake and so eat less of them. However, this is a short-lived trigger to stop eating. If the food is prevented from entering the stomach and being digested (e.g. in an animal which has a tube in their oesophagus that removes the swallowed food) an animal will eat a normal-sized meal but will return to eat another meal shortly afterwards (Janowitz and Grossman 1949).

Stomach

As we eat our stomach expands (distends). Many researchers believe that we have receptors in the stomach that monitor the degree of distension and that this acts as a trigger to stop eating. To test this, Geliebter *et al.* (1987) filled one third of rats' stomachs with water-filled balloons and found that the rats ate smaller meals. In another study, the vagus nerve (which sends information about stomach distension to the brain) was cut (Gonzalez and Deutsch 1981). In this case the animals ate until they had overfilled their stomachs.

Intestines

Once food has been mixed with hydrochloric acid and pepsin (an enzyme) in the stomach it passes slowly into the intestines. A satiety mechanism here is the release of a hormone called **cholecystokinin (CCK)**. This hormone causes the gallbladder to contract, releasing bile into the intestine. The relevance of CCK is that its levels in the blood change with the amount of food in the intestines. Hence a high level of CCK in the blood will signal that food is being digested. Evidence for this comes from studies that have shown that injections of CCK will suppress eating (Gibbs 1973). In addition there are known to be CCK receptors in the intestine and these may send signals to the brain via the vagus nerve.

Liver

We have already seen that the liver monitors the level of glucose and free fatty acids by monitoring how well its own energy requirements are met. When blood glucose levels are high (soon after eating a meal), the liver will signal to the brain that there is no immediate need for eating.

Summary of eating mechanisms

We have seen that there are a number of mechanisms that signal that we need to eat and that we have eaten enough. It is not surprising that there are different monitors around the body as there is a considerable time lag between the act of eating and the benefits gained from it. In some senses we have to best guess that we are going to be lacking in energy a short time in the future. Having a number of ways to assess the situation ensures that we never get so short of energy that we cannot function properly. Having said that, we are able to go without food for long periods of time without perishing. The same cannot be said for a shortage of water, and we will look next at the mechanisms that regulate the homeostatic mechanism of drinking.

Drinking

Nearly 70 per cent of our entire body is made up of water. You might think, therefore, that it would be pretty difficult to lose too much. However, the water is spread across three different compartments and it is the balance of water between these compartments that must be homeostatically maintained. Before looking at the mechanisms of thirst and drinking we will examine what these compartments are.

Water compartments

There are three types of water in the body. These are:

- water in the **intracellular fluid**

Look at the diagram below. There are six errors in it. Make a copy and correct the errors.

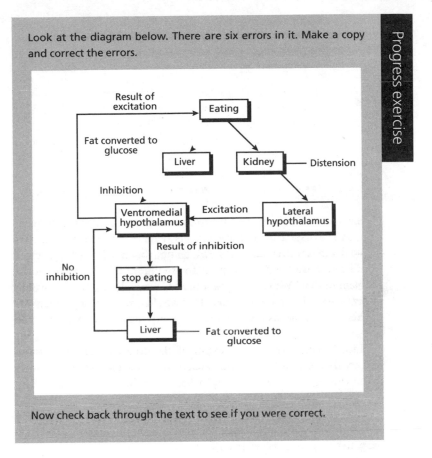

Now check back through the text to see if you were correct.

- water in the **extracellular fluid**
- water in the blood

The membranes that separate these three types of compartment are all semi-permeable. This means that they let some things pass through them but do not let others. All of them let water pass through very easily. Other chemicals, like salts, will pass through less easily (if at all). The body tries to maintain an equal concentration of these salts in all three compartments.

Consider Figure 6.1. Supposing I were to remove some water from compartment A. This would leave the concentration of salt in A

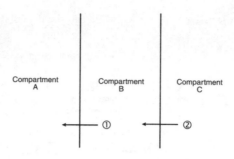

Figure 6.1 The consequence of water loss from compartment A

higher than in B. Water would flow from compartment B to compartment A to balance the concentrations (Figure 6.1①). However, this would leave a difference between compartments B and C. Water would also have to move from C to B (Figure 6.1②). Where is the problem in that? Well, if compartment C were blood, then we would be decreasing the blood pressure. This would now cause a problem for the heart which needs the pressure to pump the blood all around the body.

This, I hope, gives you a flavour of the need to maintain a water balance. Let us now look at this balance in a little more detail and add to this the mechanisms that detect when the balance is no longer being maintained. There are two types of water loss that we encounter and so there are two types of thirst. For each one we can describe the reason for the water imbalance, the mechanism of detection and how the water imbalance is removed.

Osmotic thirst

Osmotic thirst refers to the thirst we get due to a decrease in the amount of water in the intracellular fluid. It is called osmotic thirst because the pressure across a **semi-permeable membrane** is referred to as the osmotic pressure. Since losing water from inside cells changes the osmotic pressure, the resulting thirst is called osmotic thirst.

Reason for the water imbalance

Imagine that you have just eaten some ready salted crisps. Having ingested a lot of salt there will be a build up of salt outside the cells (in the extracellular fluid). Water will therefore be drawn away from the intracellular fluid in order to balance things out.

Mechanism of detection

Loss of water from a cell affects the functioning of the internal workings of that cell. For example, you are already familiar with the role of concentrations of ions inside and outside a neuron (see Chapter 2). Therefore, if water is lost from cells it must be detected rapidly. However, not all cells have the ability to signal intracellular water loss. Blass and Epstein (1971) discovered that osmotic thirst receptors are located in the preoptic nucleus of the hypothalamus. They injected salt directly into this brain region and found that this led to drinking. When they injected salt elsewhere in the brain drinking did not occur.

Removing the water imbalance

An obvious way to remove the water imbalance is to initiate drinking. However, until drinking occurs the body has another mechanism that can, at least, reduce any further imbalance. The kidneys function to regulate the amount of water and salts that we excrete via the urine. The posterior pituitary gland secretes antidiuretic hormone (ADH) into the bloodstream. This causes the kidneys to conserve water but not salts and to excrete a very concentrated urine. Osmoreceptors in the preoptic nucleus and outside of the brain may cause the secretion of ADH and thereby prevent further water imbalance.

Volumetric thirst

Volumetric thirst refers to the thirst we have when we have lost water from the blood. It is called volumetric because losing water from the blood decreases the blood volume.

Reason for the water imbalance

The most obvious cause of a loss of blood volume is due to bleeding. This causes the water in the blood to be reduced. However, it does not cause water to flow from the extracellular fluid into the blood because blood also contains salts. Losing blood, therefore, results in a loss of an **isotonic** (meaning same tension) solution. The term isotonic refers to the fact that the blood has the same concentration of salts as the rest of the body's fluids. So the result of a loss of blood is a reduced blood volume and a loss of both water and salts.

Mechanism of detection

Without a sufficient blood volume the heart cannot do its job properly. Remember, also, that the kidneys regulate the excretion of water and salts. It is not surprising, therefore, to find that there are volumetric receptors in both the heart and kidneys (Fitzsimmons 1971).

Removing the water imbalance

Receptors in the kidney detect the lowered blood volume and stimulate the adrenal glands to secrete aldosterone which inhibits the kidneys from excreting any more sodium. Furthermore, they appear to stimulate the brain to initiate the eating of salty foods. They also stimulate the posterior pituitary to secrete ADH which conserves water. The receptors in the heart appear to initiate drinking to replace the water (Fitzsimmons and Moore-Gillon 1980). The region of the brain thought to be responsible for initiating this kind of drinking is the **subfornical organ** which lies in the region of the third ventricle. These mechanisms are complicated and not fully understood.

Before we end this section, a word or two about dehydration. We lose water and/or salts from a number of sources: from our skin, from breathing, and from sweating, to name but a few. These tend to produce water loss from all three compartments and so they lead to both osmotic thirst and volumetric thirst.

Drinking satiety

As was the case for eating satiety, it is not sensible for the body to continue taking in water until the water compartments have returned to their balanced state. This would lead to a water excess. The future balance must be anticipated from the current drinking. It appears that the mouth and oesophagus, the stomach and the liver all play a role in terminating drinking behaviour, although none of these alone are sufficient to terminate drinking.

Mouth and oesophagus

At first sight the evidence concerning the role of the mouth and oesophagus appears contradictory. Injecting water directly into the stomach of a thirsty animal when it presses a lever produces normal amounts of 'drinking' (Epstein and Teitelbaum 1962). However, allowing the animal to drink normally but ensuring the water never reaches the stomach results in excessive, but not continued, drinking (Adolph 1950). It appears that water that passes through the mouth has a temporary (and small) satiation effect.

Stomach

Blass and Hall (1976) have shown that the stomach makes a small contribution to drinking satiation. They placed a noose around the opening to the intestine from the stomach. This could be closed and opened so that, when closed, water drunk could go no further than the stomach. Under these conditions thirsty animals drank more than normal but less than animals whose drinking did not enter the stomach.

Liver

There are several pieces of evidence that show that the liver is involved in the cessation of drinking. For example, Smith and Jerome (1983) cut the vagus nerve that connects the liver to the brain and showed that these animals drink more water than normal. This suggests that the vagus nerve sends signals to the brain to inhibit drinking.

Summary of drinking mechanisms

Two types of thirst can occur. Osmotic thirst arises from a loss of intracellular water and volumetric thirst arises from a loss of blood volume. Gaining or losing salts is just as important as gaining or losing water and the mechanisms work to maintain an isotonic environment.

The evidence for what causes drinking satiety is not clear. It appears that the mouth and oesophagus, stomach and liver all play some role but the relative importance of each is hard to evaluate.

Chapter summary

We have examined three homeostatic mechanisms in this chapter. All three mechanisms involve processes for detecting deviations from the set point (perhaps better conceived of as a set range) and processes for making corrections. Common to all of the mechanisms discussed here is an important role for nuclei of the hypothalamus. In addition, eating and drinking appear to involve the ANS and endocrine system as part of their control processes (temperature control only involves the ANS).

Temperature regulation is the most straightforward of the three mechanisms discussed here. The preoptic area of the hypothalamus is the major regulator of core body temperature. For eating and drinking there is more than one source of control. We have reviewed the debate over whether glucose or fat levels are the most important factor in hunger and have examined the two types of water imbalance that can lead to drinking behaviour.

The material you have read in this chapter is complicated and you will probably need to re-read it a few times. Do not be concerned if all of the material has not sunk in in one go. The fine-tuning of these processes is crucial to our existence and so you would expect the mechanisms to have the complexity required to deal with any eventuality.

Further reading

Kalat, J.W. (1998) *Biological Psychology*. 6th edn. Brooks/Cole Publishing Company, Belmont, CA. ISBN 0–534–34893–9. An excellent all-round text which deals with all three homeostatic mechanisms in a lot of detail (there is a separate chapter for each).

There is an associated internet study centre at: http://psychstudy. brookscole.com/kalat_bio.shtml
You will need a user-id and password to gain entry to the study centre but this can be obtained by your tutor.

Schneider, A.M. (1995) *Elements of Physiological Psychology*. McGraw Hill, New York, ISBN 0–07–911488–1. Chapter 11 is a very thorough and clear account of eating and drinking.

Below are a numbered set of concepts and a lettered set of explanations. See if you can correctly match the correct number with the correct letter.

1 Osmotic thirst
2 Core body temperature
3 Lipostatic theory
4 Set point
5 Volumetric thirst
6 Glucostatic theory
7 Intracellular
8 Metabolism

A The process of extraction and storage of fuels from the blood.
B The inside of cells.
C Thirst due to loss of fluid from the blood.
D Whether or not we are hungry depends on the level of blood glucose.
E The limited range of values which is ideal for any homeostatic process.
F Thirst due to loss of fluid from cells.
G Whether or not we are hungry depends on the level of free fatty acids.
H The temperature of the internal environment.

For each of the first six concepts give an example that helps to explain it. When you have finished go back to the text and check whether or not you were correct.

7

How drugs affect the brain

Introduction

In Chapter 2 we saw how an action potential travels along an axon and how this leads to the release of neurotransmitter from the terminal bouton. In this chapter you will discover how drugs alter the processes of synaptic transmission, thereby having a behavioural effect. First, let us briefly review the sequence of events at the synapse.

When an action potential reaches the terminal bouton it causes calcium ions to enter the bouton. This, in turn, leads to neurotransmitter substance being released from the bouton. The neurotransmitter enters the synaptic cleft and diffuses across to the **postsynaptic terminal**. On the postsynaptic terminal there are receptor sites. Provided that the neurotransmitter has the right shape for the postsynaptic receptor (lock and key), the neurotransmitter will attach itself to the receptor. This causes the permeability of the postsynaptic membrane to change and ions will either go in or out of the postsynaptic cell. (If any of this is not clear, then go back and re-read Chapter 2.)

With this process in mind we can first ask about the types of effect a drug could have on the functioning of the synapse.

Types of effect that could occur

There are basically only two effects that a drug can have. It can either enhance the action of the naturally occurring neurotransmitter (an agonist) or it can diminish such action (an antagonist). However, it can achieve this in a number of different ways. For example, to enhance a neurotransmitter's action the drug could cause more to be released, allow that which is released to last for longer, or prevent it from being metabolised (to name but a few). Similarly, to diminish a neurotransmitter's action the drug could cause less to be released, block the receptor site, or increase the rate at which it is metabolised (again, to name but a few).

We will look at these possibilities in detail in a moment but let me first impress upon you the importance of this consideration. Different drugs might have the same behavioural outcome by doing different things. If, for example, a decrease in the effect of a neurotransmitter is desired, one drug might block the receptor site for that neurotransmitter whilst another might prevent neurotransmitter release. They would both, nevertheless, have the same psychoactive effect. An example of this is seen in treatments for depression where different types of drug treatment produce the same outcome at the synapse (and, hence, the same behavioural change) but do so in slightly different ways.

The above might prompt you to ask why we would need more than one drug on the market. Apart from the fact that the different drugs might have different **potencies** (degrees to which they decrease the neurotransmitter effect, in our example), the mechanism by which a drug acts might determine the type of side effects that it has. One reason for this is that drugs do not work on only the synapses we wish them to. They work on all synapses of that type wherever they occur in the brain. The search for drugs which work only at the desired locations in the brain is the search for what has been termed the 'magic bullet'. Unfortunately, this has not yet been achieved for *any* drugs.

Having considered why a knowledge of how drugs work might be important, let us now look in more detail at the possible synaptic sites at which drugs can have their effect.

Possible sites for drug effects

Figure 7.1 (on p.83) shows a section through a synapse in more detail than the one we encountered in Chapter 2. Such detail is provided here only to enable you to understand the discussion that follows. There are numerous sites at which a drug can act and some of them are given below. Read the progress exercise before reading on.

Make yourself a rough copy of Figure 7.1. Then as you read about each of the possible sites for drug action mark them on the drawing.

Progress exercise

1   The neurotransmitter substance is stored in the synaptic vesicles. However, it is usually synthesised at the other end of the axon in the cell body. So the first place a drug can act is on the synthesis of the neurotransmitter itself. A drug might prevent synthesis or might enhance it by providing more of the chemicals needed for its production.

2   Although neurotransmitters are mostly synthesised in the cell body, some (e.g. noradrenaline) are produced in the bouton. Often this is because neurotransmitter molecules are broken down in the synaptic cleft and the reusable products are brought back into the cell. It is usual for enzymes to be involved in the production of neurotransmitters here and so a second way that a drug can act is to alter the activity of such enzymes.

3   A third way that a drug can act is to prevent the neurotransmitter being stored in the vesicles.

4   During normal synaptic transmission an action potential causes calcium ions to enter the bouton so as to enable the

neurotransmitter to be released. Easing or blocking this entry of calcium ions will again alter the functioning of the neuron.

5   After the neurotransmitter has been released it travels across the synaptic cleft and locks on to a postsynaptic receptor. Helping or hindering such attachment is another way in which a drug can have an effect.

6   Most neurotransmitters are broken down by **enzymes** in the synaptic cleft. Interfering with this breakdown will change the activity of the neurotransmitter.

7   Excess neurotransmitter that does not attach to a receptor site and/or breakdown products from the previous point is taken back into the terminal bouton. Blocking this action prolongs the time during which neurotransmitter can attach to a receptor site.

8   Some neurotransmitters are taken back up into the bouton as whole molecules and are broken down by enzymes in the bouton. This is another place where a psychoactive drug can have an effect.

9   There are autoreceptors on the membrane of the terminal bouton. These regulate the synthesis and release of new neurotransmitter within the neuron. They do this when neurotransmitter attaches to the autoreceptor from the outside this signals to the cell that there is excess neurotransmitter in the cleft and so no more is synthesised or released. By blocking these autoreceptors, the neuron can be fooled into thinking that there is not enough neurotransmitter and so it will produce or release some more.

These are complicated but, I hope you agree, fascinating mechanisms. You should not expect to remember them all and you should certainly not invest valuable time trying to learn them all at this stage. However, they will help you to understand the material covered in the next two chapters. To finish this chapter we will look at some drugs to see which parts of this synaptic process they affect and what the consequences are. You will meet more of them in Chapter 9.

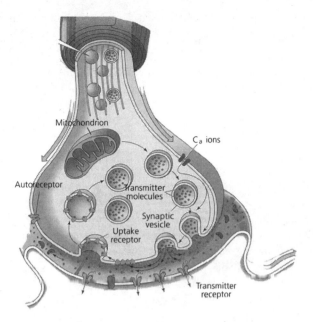

Mitochondrion

C_a ions

Autoreceptor

Transmitter molecules

Synaptic vesicle

Uptake receptor

Transmitter receptor

Figure 7.1 Section through a synapse

Examples of drugs and their synaptic effects

Diazepam

Probably one of the most well known therapeutic drugs is **diazepam** (known commonly as Valium). This drug is a **benzodiazepine**, which is a member of the class of drugs called **sedative hypnotics** (depressants). Diazepam enhances **GABA** activity and so is called a GABA agonist. The means by which it does this is by helping GABA to bind to its receptors. As GABA is an inhibitory neurotransmitter the result of taking diazepam is to increase the level of inhibition in the nervous system. This is consistent with the drug's behavioural effects, which are to calm a person down and make them less excitable. Hence this drug is often prescribed for people suffering from anxiety.

Alcohol

One of the most common recreational drugs is **alcohol**. This drug, like diazepam, is a sedative hypnotic (depressant). This does not immediately fit with our perception of drinking alcohol. On the contrary, alcohol is usually associated with merriment and increased activity, especially of those behaviours which we normally are too inhibited to produce. How, then, can we explain the behaviour we observe with the synaptic effects of the drug? There is in fact no mystery if we look closely at how alcohol works. Alcohol has several different effects but one of them is to decrease the activity of neurons all over the nervous system. At low doses, the activity of inhibitory neurons is decreased but the activity of excitatory neurons is unaffected. So the net effect on behaviour is to increase overall excitation. At higher doses these excitatory neurons are also inhibited and so, at this point, the net effect switches to an overall inhibition.

In addition, alcohol now starts to have a GABA agonist effect. Behaviourally, this has the following consequences. At low doses of alcohol the nervous system is excited and this leads us to feel merry. The lack of inhibitory effects at low doses might also be responsible for our feeling less inhibited. As the dose of alcohol gets higher the effect on behaviour is a depression. This is seen by the fact that people who have drunk too much alcohol often feel low and start crying. By the morning, we are hungover and generally feel more depressed than normal. Incidentally, it is believed that the hangover is not a GABA effect but an effect of physical dependence (Cicero 1978), a term that you will learn more about in Chapter 8.

Chapter summary

We have seen in this chapter that drugs can work at a number of different locations in the synaptic region. They can be agonists that mimic the action of the naturally occurring neurotransmitter substance or they can be antagonists that prevent the natural neurotransmitter from functioning. You have been introduced to two different drugs as examples of these various actions. In the next chapter we consider how psychoactive drugs are classified. With the knowledge gained here you should be able to appreciate how different drugs of the same class can have the same physiological effect whilst their method of action is different.

Re-read either the section on diazepam or the section on alcohol. From the information given about what part of the synapse the drug affects, write down and explain all the other synaptic sites that could be altered to achieve the same end result.

Review exercise

Further reading

Grilly, D.M. (1994) *Drugs and Human Behaviour*. Allyn & Bacon, Boston, MA. ISBN 0–205–26501–4. This provides an extremely thorough account of drug action. It is, perhaps, too detailed and technical for some students but provides plenty of accessible material for all readers.

There are not many non-technical sources of information about this topic.

8

Classifying psychoactive drugs

Introduction
Sedative hypnotics
Stimulants
Opiate narcotics
Hallucinogens and psychedelics
Antipsychotic tranquillisers
Tolerance, dependence and withdrawal

Introduction

Most of you reading this book will know someone who has had alcohol or caffeine and who has therefore used a **psychoactive drug.** A psychoactive drug can be loosely defined as any drug that causes a change in consciousness. However, this definition is too broad because, as Reber (1985) points out, such a definition would include almost any drug, including aspirin. The term is, therefore, usually employed to refer to drugs that fall into the five generally agreed classes: sedative hypnotics, stimulants, opiate narcotics, hallucinogens and psychedelics, and antipsychotic tranquillisers. It should be noted that many drugs have a different effect depending upon a number of factors such as the dose. For example, as we have seen, alcohol is classed as a depressant but can have a stimulating effect at low doses. The classification in the tables at the beginning of each class is based mainly on medical and recreational usage and therefore provides us with a useful initial starting point from which to analyse the effects of psychoactive drugs. Also included in the tables are the neurotransmitter substances that are mostly affected by the example drugs given for each class and I have also stated whether the drug acts as an agonist or an antagonist.

Sedative hypnotics

The sedative hypnotics are also sometimes referred to as **depressants**. They are a very diverse group of drugs but they all have one thing in common, namely, to depress or decrease behavioural activity. Whilst there are many drugs in this group, they all behave in exactly the same way. Depending upon the dose of the drug the effect of these drugs can be very different. At very low doses, the drugs have an **anxiolytic** effect which means that they will tend to reduce anxiety. As the dose increases the drugs cause **disinhibition**, that is, the tendency to behave in a less inhibited way. Further increases lead to **sedation** and then **hypnosis** or sleep. At relatively high doses these drugs cause **general anaesthesia**. Finally, very high doses will cause a person to go into a coma and too high a dose will cause death. In addition, it should be noted that the drugs in this class have an additive effect. So taking a dose of tranquilliser together with a dose of alcohol will produce a greater depressive effect than taking either dose alone.

Why, then, if the drugs all follow the same dose-related pattern (that is, the sequence of effects as the dosage is increased) are they used in different ways clinically and recreationally? The answer is due mainly to their potency. All the drugs follow the above pattern as the

Drugs in the group	Neurotransmitter substance affected	Agonist or antagonist
Alcohol	GABA	Agonist
Barbiturates	GABA	Agonist
Benzodiazepines	GABA	Agonist

dose of the drug increases but the actual dose required for any given drug to achieve a given level of effect will be different. For example, if a smaller amount of a **barbiturate** (e.g. phenobarbital) than a benzo-diazepine (e.g. diazepam) were to be needed to induce sleep then the barbiturate would be said to be more potent than the benzodiazepine.

There are other differences between the drugs in this group. For example, the various drugs differ in their **dependence** and **tolerance**. These two terms will be defined and discussed fully later in the chapter, but for now we can simply define dependence as the need to keep taking the drug and tolerance as the need to take a higher and higher dose over time to get the same effect.

Stimulants

In direct contrast to the sedative hypnotics, **stimulants** lead to an increase in behavioural activity. Also in contrast with the sedative hypnotics, the different drugs in this class work on different neuro-transmitters and in very different ways. For example, **amphetamine** resembles noradrenaline and so mimics it and acts directly on **nora-drenergic** (the -ergic ending means using that neurotransmitter – hence noradrenergic means using noradrenaline) receptors. **Cocaine** also affects the same receptors but it perpetuates the action of nora-drenaline itself by blocking its reuptake into the presynaptic terminal (see Chapter 7 for details on the different synaptic actions of drugs). By contrast, **nicotine** acts at the receptor sites of some **acetylcholine** synapses.

Drugs in the group	Neurotransmitter substance affected	Agonist or antagonist
Amphetamine	Dopamine, noradrenaline	Agonist
Cocaine	Dopamine, noradrenaline	Agonist
Antidepressants	Serotonin (5HT), nora-drenaline	Agonist
Caffeine	Noradrenaline	Agonist
Nicotine	Acetylcholine	Agonist

Amphetamine and cocaine in low doses affect behaviour by elevating mood, increasing alertness and decreasing fatigue. They can even induce a sense of euphoria. At high doses they can cause irritability, anxiety and even psychotic behaviour. Amphetamine has some clinical uses such as alleviating asthma (because it causes dilation of the air passages of the lungs), the symptoms of **Parkinson's disease** and hyperkinesis (excessive and inappropriate motor activity) in children. It was at one time used in controlling obesity as it has an appetite suppressant effect. However, it is no longer used because tolerance to this effect occurs rapidly and so the dose has to be increased. This can lead to the problems with higher doses mentioned above.

Cocaine, as well as having the same general effects as amphetamine is also a potent local anaesthetic at low doses. Consequently, cocaine users often anaesthetise their nose when using the drug. Cocaine has no clinical uses, probably because (unlike amphetamine) it only remains active in the body for a few minutes as it is metabolised by the liver extremely quickly.

We will discuss the **antidepressants** in more detail later in this chapter. Suffice it to say here that reversing depression is an obvious effect of stimulant drugs. What marks stimulants and antidepressants as particularly useful for their task is that they tend to specifically stimulate noradrenergic and **serotonergic** neurons which are known to be affected in depression. Moreover, these drugs tend not to be used for recreational purposes as, for some unknown reason, they have little behavioural effect on non-depressed people.

Caffeine is the most widely used stimulant in the world. It acts on an enzyme found in noradrenergic neurons and increases the rate of cellular metabolism thereby exciting the cell. It affects the cerebral cortex first (lower doses) and causes increased mental alertness, wakefulness and restlessness. In higher doses it also affects the brainstem and can increase respiration and the output from the heart. Massive doses, equivalent to around 25 cups of coffee in one go, will cause convulsions. Clinically it can be used to relieve migraine headaches because it constricts the brain's blood vessels.

Nicotine is the second most widely used drug. It stimulates all levels of the nervous system. As well as having a generalised stimulant effect (increasing levels of behavioural activity), nicotine also reduces muscle tone and it is probably this action that causes smokers to feel more relaxed when they have a cigarette.

> The sedative hypnotics and stimulants have opposing behavioural effects. From the text above, list as many of the differences between them as you can. Now read the descriptions of the other classes and then decide whether they are more like the sedative hypnotics, more like the stimulants, or very different from either of them.

Progress exercise

Opiate narcotics

The term **narcotic** is used to refer to any drug that has both sedative and **analgesic** (pain-relieving) properties. The only drugs which fulfil this requirement are the naturally occurring or synthetically made opiates.

The natural drugs that can be extracted from the opium poppy are morphine and codeine. The most well known of the synthesised compounds is, of course, heroin. All the opiates have a medical use in the relief of pain, the treatment of diarrhoea and the suppression of coughs. However, for most of them their addictive nature makes them risky to use in any but the severest situations. Codeine is much more widely used as it is far less potent than morphine.

Drugs in the group	Neurotransmitter substance affected	Agonist or antagonist
Morphine	Enkephalins and endorphins	Agonist
Heroin	Enkephalins and endorphins	Agonist

The opiate narcotics work by mimicking the action of the endogenous (meaning occurring naturally within us) opiates which are the **enkephalins** and **endorphins**. Drugs like heroin are very potent and cause a feeling of intense pleasure when injected. This suggests that the endogenous opiates must have a natural analgesic and a reward/pleasure role. Indeed, it is believed that the high obtained after, say, dancing the night away is due to the natural release of these endogenous opiates.

Hallucinogens and psychedelics

This class of drugs causes disturbances in perception and cognition and can give rise to auditory or visual hallucinations. The drugs have a wide variety of chemical structures and affect a number of different neurotransmitters. For example, **physostigmine** causes an increase in the amount of ACh available at its synapses and can induce a wide variety of **psychobehavioural** effects such as nightmares, hallucinations and decreased intellectual functioning. **Mescaline**, on the other hand, is an noradrenaline agonist with similar general effects to amphetamine (discussed above). However, mescaline produces strong visual hallucinations which amphetamine rarely does except at very high doses.

Probably the most well known psychedelic drug is **lysergic acid diethylamide (LSD)**. It is a serotonin agonist at most brain sites although it has been shown to be an antagonist at a few. Contrary to popular belief, physical dependence does not develop although

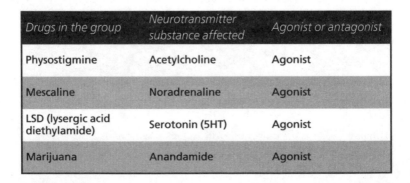

Drugs in the group	Neurotransmitter substance affected	Agonist or antagonist
Physostigmine	Acetylcholine	Agonist
Mescaline	Noradrenaline	Agonist
LSD (lysergic acid diethylamide)	Serotonin (5HT)	Agonist
Marijuana	Anandamide	Agonist

psychological dependence and tolerance can occur. LSD is a synthetically made drug and, whilst it has general psychedelic properties, the precise effects on the user are unpredictable. Its effects seem to be influenced by personality, expectations and mood of the user as well as the setting in which the drug is taken. The most common experience is one of marked alterations in mood and emotion. Sadness or laughter can be intense and a sense of euphoria or dysphoria can be experienced. In addition, the user will most probably experience visual hallucinations.

Marijuana is a drug derived from the plant *Cannabis sativa*. The psychoactive compound found in these plants is **tetrahydrocannabinol (THC)**. Marijuana appears to act as an agonist at naturally occurring THC receptors for which the endogenous neurotransmitter is **anandamide**. Its place within this class of drugs is somewhat strange because at normal doses it resembles more the sedative-hypnotic effects of alcohol. Only at high doses is it mildly hallucinogenic with a potency similar to a mild dose of LSD. At normal (social) doses, THC causes minor mood alterations. At higher doses these alterations become intensified but the individual remains in full control and any behavioural changes are not likely to be noticed. However, mild sensory distortions and hallucinations may be experienced. It is only with extremely high doses that more pronounced hallucinations and loss of control are likely to occur. As with LSD, physical dependence does not develop but, unlike LSD, neither does THC tolerance.

Antipsychotic tranquillisers

Drugs in the group	Neurotransmitter substance affected	Agonist or antagonist
Chlorpromazine	Dopamine/ noradrenaline	Antagonist
Reserpine	Noradrenaline	Antagonist
Lithium	Noradrenaline	Antagonist

Only a brief outline of this class is presented here as they are discussed more fully later in the chapter. The **antipsychotic tranquillisers** (also sometimes known as the **major tranquillisers**) can calm the psychotic patient in a way that cannot be achieved using sedative-hypnotics or minor tranquillisers. Whilst the sedative-hypnotics are useful in treating anxiety and neuroticism, and the antidepressants are useful for many types of depression, only the antipsychotic tranquillisers can be used to treat true psychoses such as schizophrenia and manic-depression. It should also be noted that the term tranquilliser, as used here, does not refer to the induction of a state of pleasant calm, but rather to a reduction in psychotic behaviour. Indeed, the psychological effects of these drugs are anything but pleasant and may be very unpleasant if taken by non-psychotic people. For this reason these drugs are seldom abused in the way that many of the other drugs we have considered are.

The most widely used subclass is the group called the **phenothiazines**, of which **chlorpromazine** is the most common. The exact mechanism by which these drugs work is not clear but they are thought to block dopamine and noradrenaline receptors. Chlorpromazine tends to suppress emotion and so produces an indifference to external stimuli. It is widely used in the treatment of **schizophrenia. Reserpine** is a drug previously used to treat psychoses. It works by blocking the uptake of noradrenaline into the synaptic vesicles inside the presynaptic terminal. The free-floating noradrenaline in the presynaptic terminal is then metabolised by **monoamine oxidase**. In this way it depletes noradrenergic neurons of noradrenaline. Reserpine is never used today because of its depressive effects. Both chlorpromazine and reserpine reduce the level of noradrenaline activity. However, because chlorpromazine does not lower the level of circulating noradrenaline (it merely prevents its action at the postsynaptic terminal), it tends not to produce depression as a side effect. **Lithium** is the treatment of choice for mania. Little is known about its mechanism of action but it is believed to prevent the release of noradrenaline from the presynaptic terminal.

Tolerance, dependence and withdrawal

In the final section of this chapter we examine why it is that drugs can become ineffective and/or addictive. An understanding of tolerance and dependence gives us an insight into how drugs work and why drug abuse might occur.

Tolerance

After repeated exposure to a drug, a person may notice a decreased response to the same dosage. This is called **drug tolerance**. The consequence of tolerance is that the dose must be increased for the same effect to be experienced. The effect of tolerance might even extend to a decreased sensitivity to another drug (a phenomenon called **cross-tolerance**). Tolerance is a problem because most of the psychoactive drugs that we take are safe in the doses normally prescribed but can be toxic at higher doses. If tolerance leads to a need for higher doses then this can become dangerous.

There are two types of tolerance, **pharmacodynamic tolerance** and **behavioural tolerance**. The former may develop for a number of reasons but a common one is that the liver comes to metabolise the drug more quickly, thereby lessening its effect with repeated use. The latter often occurs as a consequence of learning. The drug develops tolerance when taken in one context but has its original effect if the context is changed. The following example might help to explain this.

Many people claim that they are better darts players when they have had a drink or two. However, alcohol is known to decrease motor performance. Such claims might not be the result of kidology but rather the result of behavioural tolerance. Taking alcohol regularly when playing darts allows for the learning (through conditioning) of compensatory behaviours that offset the performance detriment due to the alcohol. As a result we begin to find that our darts-playing remains 'competent' with increasing amounts of alcohol. Add to this the effect of practice and it may appear that alcohol actually improves our performance. However, we should note that such tolerance effects only extend to similar types of behaviour (generalisation) and would not result in, say, a better driving performance.

Dependence and withdrawal

When a person compulsively continues to use a drug even though it is having adverse effects we say that the person has developed a **drug**

dependence. This should be distinguished from drug abuse where there need not be any compulsivity attached. As with tolerance, there are two forms of dependence, **psychological dependence** and **physiological dependence**. The former results from a compulsion to take the drug because of the pleasure that is derived from it. This compulsion might be linked to the reward centres in the brain. Olds and Milner (1954) discovered areas in the hindbrain, midbrain and forebrain that appeared to be part of a brain reward system. It is now believed that many of the drugs for which psychological dependence develops act to excite part or all of this reward system. This is especially true of cocaine and amphetamine.

Physical dependence is closely linked to withdrawal. It is characterised by the fact that adverse physical symptoms occur when the drug is withheld after prolonged use. The withdrawal effects are usually the reverse of the effects of the drug itself. So, for example, whereas barbiturates are calming and sleep-inducing, withdrawal results in anxiety and wakefulness.

Physical dependence can sometimes lead to a psychological dependence as the person develops a compulsion to take the drug in order to avert the adverse effects of withdrawal. However, this is not always the case and depends on the psychological context of the drug. If, for instance, the drug being taken is an antidepressant then physical dependence might be offset by a psychological desire not to be on the drugs for the rest of one's life.

Chapter summary

In this chapter we have looked at the five classes of psychoactive drugs. There are similarities between some of the classes in that they have effects on identical neurotransmitter systems. The difference between such classes is often the potency of the drugs and therefore the intensity of the effect. We have also looked in this chapter at tolerance, dependence and withdrawal, which can be a problem with some, but not all, of the drugs used both therapeutically and recreationally.

Without referring back to the text, write down one example of a drug from each class. For each drug state the neurotransmitter it acts upon and a little bit about its uses.

Now go back and check the text to see how accurate you were.

Review exercise

Further reading

Grilly, D.M. (1994) *Drugs and Human Behaviour*. Allyn & Bacon, Boston, MA. ISBN 0–205–26501–4. This provides an extremely detailed account of the classifications of drugs. It is, perhaps, too detailed and technical for some students but provides plenty of accessible material for all readers.

Drugs and behaviour

Introduction

It would take a book larger than this one to describe and evaluate the variety of psychoactive drugs described in the previous chapter. Instead, this chapter concentrates on just two subclasses, antidepressants and antipsychotics. For each, the behavioural symptoms of the disorder are described, the major biological hypothesis is discussed and the available drugs are evaluated.

Depression and the antidepressants

In the previous chapter we looked very briefly at antidepressants. Before we can look more closely at their physiological and psychological actions it is useful to explore the behavioural manifestation of clinical depression and the current theory concerning the physiology of **depression**. We also need to characterise the different types of depression.

Types of depression

The first way that we can separate depression into types is by considering the source of the depression. We all become depressed from time to time, especially in reaction to life events, and this type of depression is called **reactive depression**. However, this is not the same as the **endogenous depression** of clinical disorders, and it is this type of depression that we focus on here. Another dimension along which depression can be characterised is by considering whether or not depression is the only manifested psychological dysfunction. Hence we can distinguish between **unipolar depression**, in which the depressive episodes occur on their own, and **bipolar depression**, in which the depressive episodes are accompanied by periods of mania. We will only consider unipolar depression here as only this form responds to antidepressant treatment. Manic depression will be considered later in the chapter when we look more closely at the antipsychotic tranquillisers (also referred to as neuroleptics).

Features of depression

When depressed, a patient will feel sad and rejected. They will also suffer a number of cognitive deficits. For example, they may lack motivation, have slower thought processes and lack self esteem (Miller 1975). In addition, they are likely to have disturbed sleeping patterns (difficulty in getting to sleep and early waking) and disturbed eating patterns (losing interest in both cooking and eating food).

Endogenous depression is episodic, with bouts of depression alternating with normal behaviour. If untreated, the periods of depression will get longer and longer and the interludes of non-depression will become shorter. Whilst our knowledge of the synaptic processes that lead to depression is relatively good, the reasons for this periodicity are poorly understood.

It is believed that endogenous depression is, to some degree, inherited. A lot of the evidence comes from adoption and twin studies. For example, Mendelwicz and Ranier (1977) showed that patients with bipolar depression who had been adopted at birth were more likely to have natural parents who suffered from depression than adoptive parents. This implies that a full understanding of the causes of depression will ultimately involve some form of genetic as well as physiological account. You might like to bear in mind these shortfalls in our understanding as we turn now to an explanation of the physiological basis of depression.

The monoamine theory of depression

The best current theory concerning the basis of depression came about pretty much by accident. In the 1950s reserpine was being used to treat high blood pressure (hypertension) because constriction of the blood vessels was known to be caused by noradrenaline (an autonomic nervous system response) and reserpine was known to deplete noradrenaline (and other catecholamine neurotransmitters) from neurons. However, in about 20 per cent of treated patients a severe depression developed. This led to the suggestion that catecholamine depletion was the root cause of depression. This is still our best explanation and drug treatments concentrate on maintaining elevated levels of catecholamines in the nervous system. It should be noted, however, that this theory is incomplete as 80 per cent of those given reserpine treatment for hypertension did not develop depression. It is likely that the causes of depression are diverse and that a low level of catecholamines is only one of the causes. Nevertheless, it is this theory that we will concentrate on in the rest of this section.

Drug treatments of depression

Having identified that catecholamine levels were critical in at least some forms of depression, the question of which one(s) arose. As you may remember from Chapter 2, there are three major catecholamines in the CNS: noradrenaline, dopamine and serotonin. Antidepressant drugs are designed to elevate one or more of these neurotransmitters. The first group of drugs are the **monoamine oxidase inhibitors** (MAOIs). In Chapter 2 we discussed how the catecholamines were inactivated in the synaptic cleft by an enzyme called monoamine oxidase. As their name suggests, the MAOIs inhibit this enzyme and so prolong the effectiveness of the naturally released neurotransmitter substance. An example of this class of drugs is **iproniazid**, which was discovered while being used to treat tuberculosis. Like the other MAOIs, iproniazid is a moderately effective antidepressant. However, this group of drugs has a wide variety of adverse side effects, probably because the increase in catecholamine activity is indiscriminate and widespread. This led to the development of a second class of drugs called the **tricyclic antidepressants** (also known as the reuptake blockers). These drugs also prolong the effectiveness of the catecholamine neurotransmitters but do so by preventing them from being taken back into the presynaptic terminal. Whilst the original drugs of this class were also indiscriminate, recent advances have led to tricyclics that are specific to either noradrenaline or serotonin. Some patients respond better to the former and some to the latter. This suggests that depression is a heterogeneous disorder.

There is a third class of antidepressant drugs called the lithium salts. These are used mainly in the treatment of mania and so are used with manic-depressives. We will look at the use of these drugs in the final section of this chapter.

Before completing this section on depression and antidepressants, I should make mention of one other form of treatment. This is the use of **electroconvulsive therapy (ECT)**. This is generally used only for cases of depression that do not respond to drug treatments. Whilst you may have heard horror stories about this treatment (or seen the film *One Flew Over the Cuckoo's Nest*), it is given in a much more humane way today, using muscle relaxants to lessen the effects of the shock. Moreover, the treatment works very well and has few side effects other than confusion and a mild amnesia for a short period immediately after the shock delivery. Indeed, even this can be reduced if the shock is delivered solely to the right hemisphere, without lessening the effectiveness of the treatment. What makes this treatment important is that it too fits in with the catecholamine hypothesis. It is suggested that ECT works by stimulating noradrenaline receptors (Heninger and Charney 1987). The exact mechanism of why this has long term effects is beyond the scope of this text but concerns a long-term change in the noradrenaline receptors that means that a small amount of noradrenaline produces a larger postsynaptic response than it did before the ECT was administered.

Find a friend who is not doing psychology. Explain to them about the different types of antidepressant and how they work.

Progress exercise

Schizophrenia and the antipsychotics

We looked earlier at a broad range of antipsychotic tranquillisers. In this section we will look specifically at those drugs used to treat schizophrenia. As for the section on antidepressants, we will start by looking at the behaviour of schizophrenics, then examine the main physiological theory of schizophrenia and then evaluate the treatment drugs.

Features of schizophrenia

It was Kraepelin (1919) who provided the first modern day characterisation of dementia praecox (he had first used the term in 1898). He described many forms of the illness but they all had a number of behavioural features in common. Among these were bizarre thoughts, paranoid and grandiose delusions, and auditory hallucinations. Around the same time, Bleuler (1911) was also studying the disorder: along with coining the term schizophrenia, he argued that it was not really a **dementia**. He also put more emphasis on the flattened emotions characteristic of the illness. Nowadays, we recognise that schizophrenia has two separate groups of symptoms: positive and negative. The **positive symptoms** refer to the disturbed thoughts, hallucinations and delusions; the **negative symptoms** refer to the emotional and social withdrawal and flattened emotions.

The disturbed thoughts of schizophrenia often manifest themselves as unlinked changes of topic when talking. So, for example, a patient will be talking about a holiday and will then, for no apparent reason and with no warning, switch to the topic of a TV chat show.

As already stated, the hallucinations are usually auditory. The voices they hear tend to either be issuing bizarre commands or passing comments and criticisms concerning the patients' behaviour. The delusions are, likewise, often bizarre and can involve both delusions of persecution and delusions of identity.

The negative symptoms of schizophrenia generally concern mood and are, as already described, characterised by a lack of emotion. However, some schizophrenics also suffer from inappropriate responses as a consequence of misperceiving the emotions of others.

The dopamine hypothesis of schizophrenia

The major hypothesis concerning schizophrenia is called the **dopamine hypothesis**. As its name suggests, this theory states that the cause of schizophrenia is an imbalance in the levels of dopamine (a catecholamine neurotransmitter) in the brain. This imbalance is deemed to take the form of an excess of dopamine. This is in direct contrast to the cause of Parkinson's disease which is an underactivity of dopamine. It is not surprising, therefore, that drugs that aid Parkinson's disease can lead to schizophrenia-like symptoms and drugs which aid schizophrenia can result in Parkinsonian symptoms. This relationship between the two diseases provides strong evidence that the dopamine theory of schizophrenia has some validity. The other evidence is that drugs used to treat schizophrenia all have in common the ability to reduce dopamine activity.

It would be wrong to believe that schizophrenia was simply the result of dopamine excess. There is a lot of evidence that it is partly the result of genetic factors and stress factors as well.[1] For example, the genetic link comes from the fact that schizophrenia is far more likely to develop in the children of a schizophrenic parent than in the rest of the population (13 times more likely). For our purposes here we can use the dopamine hypothesis to examine how and why the drug treatments for schizophrenia work.

---

1 See *Psychopathology* in this series for details of these other factors.

The serotonin link

Serotonin is another monoamine and is linked to dopamine through its ability to inhibit dopamine activity. The precise mechanism is unclear but this link suggests that a drug (or combination of drugs) that lowers levels of dopamine and increases the activity of serotonin ought to prove a better treatment for schizophrenics than lowering dopamine alone.

Drug therapies of schizophrenia

If schizophrenia involves an excess of dopamine then we would expect drug treatments to lower the dopamine level. One of the first drugs to be found to help schizophrenics was chlorpromazine (discovered by Henri Laborit in the 1940s). At that time it was not known why chlorpromazine worked, simply that it did. We now know that what this drug does is to block dopamine receptors in the brain. It prevents some of the dopamine released at presynaptic boutons from acting and thereby controls the dopamine excess.

Chlorpromazine is a relatively low potency **neuroleptic**. A high potency neuroleptic is **haloperidol**. It would appear that the potency differences reflect a difference in the proportion of dopamine receptors that are inhibited. Hence the high potency neuroleptics tend to be better at reducing more severe forms of schizophrenia. However, it has been shown that when neuroleptics are taken along with an enhancer of serotonin activity (e.g. Prozac), the combined effect is often greater than the effect of the individual neuroleptic. Alternatively, there is a drug that increases serotonin activity as well as reducing dopamine activity. This drug is called clozapine. Given that clozapine does not block as many dopamine receptors as, say, haloperidol does you might expect a reduced antipsychotic effect. However, clozapine is more selective in the types of dopamine receptor that are blocked (seemingly, the receptors that are blocked are those responsible for schizophrenia).

There are some serious limitations to the drug treatment of schizophrenia. For a start, not all patients respond to the drugs. Secondly, the drugs have a number of associated side effects. Whilst for most users these are merely irritating (e.g. dry mouth and blurred vision), for some they can be the development of **tardive dyskinesia**. This is a condition associated with involuntary movements of the muscles. However, the real mystery is why tardive dyskinesia develops at all. If the dopamine theory of schizophrenia is correct then the last side effect a patient should suffer from when taking drugs to reduce the level of dopamine is a condition caused by an excess of dopamine. The solution to this mystery has not fully unfolded yet but may well involve receptor supersensitivity. Tardive dyskinesia tends to occur in patients who have been taking neuroleptics for a long time. It would seem that prolonged use results in an increased sensitivity of the remaining available dopamine receptors. This hypothesis has some support from the fact that increasing the neuroleptic dose reduces the level of tardive dyskinesia.

The treatment of manic depression

The ability of lithium carbonate to reduce the symptoms of **manic depression** has been long established (Cade 1949). As I have stated before, the exact mechanism is not known. However, it has been hypothesised that the cause of the fluctuations between mania and depression may be due to alterations in the levels of neurotransmitter in the relevant neurons. That is, sometimes the presynaptic membrane may let in too much neurotransmitter and the result is manic behaviour. At other times too little might be let in, resulting in depression. If this is the case then we might surmise that lithium salts have the capacity to stabilise the membrane in some way.

Chapter summary

In this chapter we have seen that the major theory of depression suggests a decrease in the availability of one or more monoamine neurotransmitters. The treatments all try to raise the levels of available neurotransmitter but do so in a variety of ways. Schizophrenia, on the other hand, is believed to be due to an excessive amount of dopamine. Treatments for this disorder all try to reduce the effect of dopamine at its receptor sites.

For each of the following statements delete the incorrect term.

Schizophrenia is believed to be the result of a(n) *shortage/excess* of dopamine.

The everyday depression that we are all prone to feeling is called *reactive/endogenous* depression.

Manic depression is a *unipolar/bipolar* disorder.

Hallucinations are a *negative/positive* symptom of schizophrenia.

Drugs that prevent the reuptake of monoamines are called *MAOIs/Tricyclics*.

Clorpromazine is a *low/high* potency neuroleptic.

ECT works on *noradrenaline/dopamine* receptors.

Tardive dyskinesia is believed to sometimes accompany the treatment of schizophrenia because the remaining, unblocked dopamine receptors become *insensitive/supersensitive*.

Further reading

Grilly, D.M. (1994) *Drugs and Human Behaviour*. Allyn & Bacon, Boston, MA. ISBN 0–205–26501–4. This provides an extremely detailed account of the antidepressants and neuroleptics. It is, perhaps, too detailed and technical for some students but provides plenty of accessible material for all readers.

Holmes, D.S. (1994) *Abnormal Psychology*. 2nd edn. Harper Collins, London. ISBN 0–673–46909–3. This is an outstanding text that is extremely easy to follow. The chapters are long and contain far more material than you need.

10

Study aids

IMPROVING YOUR ESSAY WRITING SKILLS

At this point in the book you have acquired the knowledge necessary
to tackle the exam itself. Answering exam questions is a skill which
this chapter shows you how to improve. Examiners have some ideas
about what goes wrong in exams. Most importantly, students do not
provide the kind of evidence the examiner is looking for. A grade C
answer is typically accurate but has limited detail and commentary,
and it is reasonably constructed. To lift such an answer to a grade A or
B may require no more than fuller detail, better use of material and a
coherent organisation. By studying the essays presented in this
chapter, and the examiner's comments, you can learn how to turn
grade C answers into grade A. Please note that marks given by the
examiner in practice essays should be used as a guide only and are not
definitive. They represent the 'raw marks' given by an AEB examiner.
That is, the marks the examiner would give to the examining board
based on a total of 24 marks per question broken down into Skill A
(description) and Skill B (evaluation). Tables showing this scheme are
in Appendix C of Paul Humphreys' title in this series, *Exam Success
in AEB Psychology*. They may not be the marks given on the examination certificate received ultimately by the student because all
examining boards are required to use a common standardised system

called the Uniform Mark Scale (UMS) which adjusts all raw scores to a single standard acceptable to all examining boards.

The essays are about the length a student would be able to write in 35–40 minutes (leaving you extra time for planning and checking). Each essay is followed by detailed comments about its strengths and weaknesses. The most common problems to look out for are:

- Failure to answer the actual question set and presenting 'one written during your course'.
- A lack of evaluation, or commentary – many weak essays suffer from this.
- Too much evaluation and not enough description. Description is vital in demonstrating your knowledge and understanding of the selected topic.
- Writing 'everything you know' in the hope that something will get credit. Excellence is displayed through selectivity, and therefore improvements can often be made by *removing* material which is irrelevant to the question set.

For more ideas on how to write good essays you should consult *Exam Success in AEB Psychology* (Paul Humphreys) in this series.

Practice essay 1

(a) Describe the organisation of the autonomic nervous system. (12 marks)

(b) Assess the influence of the autonomic nervous system on any one behavioural function. (12 marks)   [AEB 1997]

Candidate's answers

(a) The autonomic nervous system (ANS) is divided up into two parts. One part is the sympathetic nervous system and the other part is the parasympathetic nervous system. The two systems work in opposite ways. For example, the sympathetic nervous system causes the heart to beat faster whereas the parasympathetic nervous system causes it to beat slower.

The parasympathetic nervous system starts in the hypothalamus and the neurons go almost to the effector organ before synapsing. Another neuron then goes to the end organ. The neurotransmitter substance released at the terminal of the second neuron is acetylcholine (ACh). For the sympathetic nervous system the neurons leave the hypothalamus and go down the spinal cord. As they leave the spinal cord they synapse at a ganglion. There is then a longer second neuron that goes to the end organ.

In general, the sympathetic nervous system prepares you for some form of activity whereas the parasympathetic nervous system calms you down again after the activity is over.

Control of the ANS in the brain is performed by the hypothalamus. The posterior and anterior nuclei are responsible for this control and these nuclei send messages to the medulla oblongata where control over things like heart rate is situated.

(b) The behavioural function I am going to talk about is the 'fight or flight' situation. This is when we are under threat and have to decide either to fight or to run away. Under these conditions the sympathetic nervous system comes into play. It raises the heart rate so that blood containing nutrients and oxygen can be sent around the body more quickly.

The sympathetic nervous system also causes some blood vessels to grow smaller. The blood to the skin is lessened so that if you are wounded during the fight you will not bleed to death. The blood is also diverted away from the stomach as you have no need to digest food. More blood is pumped to the muscles so that they can keep going either in fighting or running away. The breathing rate also increases so that more oxygen can be taken into the blood. The pupils are dilated so that you can see more accurately.

The autonomic nervous system is of vital importance in such a situation. The body needs to be in the best possible condition for both attacking and defending. In attacking, good eyesight and plenty of energy to muscles will enable you to put up a good fight or to run away faster and for longer. Taking blood away from the skin prevents you losing too much blood should you be injured.

After the danger is over, the parasympathetic nervous system restores the body to its normal levels of functioning. The heart rate and blood pressure decrease, blood vessels to the limbs constrict and digestion is restarted (to name a few). It is important that the body's functions are restored to their normal levels because if this did not happen then illness could result. This is why we get heart disease and immune diseases when we are stressed. The link here is that the fight or flight response is equivalent to the alarm phase of Selye's general adaptation syndrome.

Examiner's comments

The answer to (a) above provides some detail of the organisation of the ANS but there is a lot of description missing. For example, it would have been nice to see a specific example of a ganglion and its end organ. Also, only one neurotransmitter substance is mentioned in relation to the system. The fact that noradrenaline is released from postganglionic sympathetic neurons has been omitted. There is an attempt to describe the role of the hypothalamus but what these hypothalamic nuclei do and how is omitted.

The question asks specifically about organisation but the answer does not really address this very well. For example, the fact that the system is, to some degree, self-monitoring via feedback mechanisms has been omitted.

In part (b) the fight or flight example is a good one and the description of what happens is not all that bad. However, the answer concentrates on the sympathetic nervous system and says little of the relative lack of a role for the parasympathetic nervous system during the actual fight or flight phase. Its role after the danger has passed has only briefly been mentioned. Of the detail on describing what happens there is an important key omission. There is no mention of the adrenal medulla and the release of adrenaline.

The assessment of the influence of the ANS is weak. The answer does try to suggest how vital the ANS is at this time but this is a little repetitious of the material used in the description. There are few references for research in this area given in textbooks but there are sufficient functions of the ANS for most of them to be examined as to the role they play in this situation. The link at the end to Selye's general adaptation syndrome is a good one but needed to be elaborated upon.

The final mark for this question is about 8 (description) + around 7 (evaluation) = 15/24 (likely to be equivalent to a grade B at A level).

Practice essay 2

(a) **Explain what is meant by the term homeostasis. (6 marks)**

(b) **Outline how the nervous system is involved in any one homeostatic function. (6 marks)**

(c) **Evaluate the involvement of the nervous system in this homeostatic function. (12 marks)** **[AEB 1998]**

Candidate's answer

(a) Homeostasis is the process by which an organism maintains a steady state. The term comes from Walter Cannon and actually means 'same state'. An organism has to maintain a constant internal environment and this is a bit like the role of a thermostat. So an organism will have a mechanism for regulating temperature. Another example would be the regulation of blood sugar levels.

(b) One example of the nervous system's involvement is body temperature. There is a temperature regulation centre in the brain. This is in a structure called the hypothalamus. It consists of a 'hot' and 'cold' centre which has heat-sensitive neurons. In cold weather, a number of responses of the hypothalamus lead to heat production. These include reduced sweating and vasodilation of the blood vessels in the skin.

(c) The hypothalamus is not the only thing involved in temperature regulation. The endocrine system is also involved. Also, the nervous system relies on things like shivering when we are cold. It is also possible to put on warm clothes or move to a warmer place. However, as mammals are warm-blooded animals they do not need to do as much to keep themselves warm as their nervous system can do most of what is needed. There is a distinct advantage to being warm-blooded as these animals are able to hunt for food even when the weather is not so warm. However, sometimes even the fact that we are warm-blooded and can regulate our body temperature does not help: for example, when we have a fever.

Examiner's comments

Part (a) is quite well answered as it shows that the candidate has a clear idea of what homeostasis means. What it lacks is a fluent elaboration of the sorts of processes that are regulated by homeostatic mechanisms. Whilst the candidate does give a couple of examples, they are not expanded upon to show that s/he knows in what way these are under homeostatic control.

Part (b) is rather brief. Whilst the hypothalamus is correctly mentioned, as is the fact that it has a 'hot' and a 'cold' centre, there is too little detail about how these regulate temperature. Only the response to cold weather is mentioned and the point about vasodilation is incorrect and would not attract any marks. One would expect to see both the response to heat and to cold mentioned. Also, the fact that this is a negative feedback mechanism is not mentioned.

You should also note that shivering is referred to in part (c). Since this is really a nervous system response to the cold, an examiner might prefer to credit this to part (b) rather than accept it as an evaluation point.

Part (c) is again quite short but the points made are good evaluative statements. It is not clear that the endocrine system is involved in temperature regulation (this would be a good point for most other homeostatic mechanisms) and, even if it were, this statement without further comment is unlikely to attract many marks. The fact that we put warm clothes on is a very good point.

The next section about warm-blooded animals is well expressed but lacks the contrast with cold-blooded animals that would attract an A grade. Likewise, the problems that we face when we have a fever is an excellent remark but we are left wondering what else we do to combat it (remove clothes, keep our skin bathed in tepid water to aid evaporation, rest to avoid generating heat through metabolism).

Overall, the answer is a tease. One is left with the feeling that the candidate might know this material quite well but doesn't expand on points sufficiently for us to be sure. The final mark is about 3 for part (a), around 4 for part (b) (both description), and about 6 for part (c) = 13/24 (likely to be equivalent to a grade C at A level).

Practice essay 3

Describe and evaluate research into the effects of any *two* drugs on behaviour. (24 marks)   **[AEB 1997]**

Candidate's answer

The two drugs I am going to describe and evaluate are iproniazid, an antidepressant, and chlorpromazine, an antipsychotic tranquilliser.

There are two types of depression. One type is reactive depression and this occurs when we suffer a trauma such as the death of a close relative. The other form is endogenous depression and this is the depression that can be considered to be abnormal as it occurs in the absence of any traumatic event.

The cause of depression is believed to be an underactivity of monoamines which are a type of neurotransmitter substance. The monoamine neurotransmitters consist of noradrenaline, dopamine and serotonin.

Iproniazid is a MAOI. It works at the synapse. The synapse is a region where the terminal bouton of one neuron meets the dendrites of the next neuron. Inbetween there is a small gap called the synaptic cleft. The terminal bouton has vesicles in it which contain the stored neurotransmitter. When an action potential comes along the axon the neurotransmitter is released into the cleft and travels to receptor sites on the dendrites. Here it causes ion channels to open and this results in either an EPSP or an IPSP.

Monoamine oxidase (MAO) is an enzyme that breaks down monoamine neurotransmitters and so a monoamine oxidase inhibitor (MAOI) stops MAO from working. As iproniazid is a MAOI it has this effect. By doing this it enables the neurotransmitter to work for longer and so it reverses the underactivity of monoamines in a depressed person.

Iproniazid is a very good antidepressant although it does have a number of side effects associated with it. These side effects can be quite bad. It is therefore not always used and an alternative is a tricyclic antidepressant. This does the same thing but does it differently and with fewer side effects. Iproniazid takes quite a long time to work and so ECT can be used in the meantime.

Schizophrenia is a mental disorder in which a person suffers from delusions, disordered thinking, and hallucinations. The delusions can either be delusions of grandeur in which the person might think that they are God, or delusions of persecution in which they might think that the police are after them. The hallucinations associated with schizophrenia are usually auditory rather than visual.

The cause of schizophrenia is believed to be an overactivity of dopamine. This is referred to as the dopamine hypothesis of schizophrenia. Chlorpromazine stops the overactivity of dopamine. It does this by blocking the receptor sites for dopamine and so prevents it from working.

Like iproniazid, chlorpromazine has rather bad side effects. It can also cause Parkinson's disease with prolonged use. It can also cause tardive dyskinesia. This fact is not consistent with the dopamine hypothesis of schizophrenia.

Overall, the two drugs discussed are good for helping to relieve the behavioural problems of depression and schizophrenia. However, neither of them are magic bullets and so one could criticise their use.

Examiner's comments

At first glance this looks like a very competent and A grade answer. However, the essay suffers from a very common fault. It does not answer the question very well. It is true that the answer is packed with mostly accurate information but if we analyse it paragraph by paragraph you will see where this candidate falls down. Note, though, that the candidate does not present any studies. This is perfectly acceptable as the term research includes theory, of which there is mention in the essay. Note also that physiological events are acceptable as demonstrations of behaviour.

The first paragraph is fine and accurate. The second paragraph is quite knowledgeable but is not relevant to the essay. The examiner will therefore ignore it. The third paragraph is good but there is no detail here. Where, for example is this underactivity?

The first sentence of the next paragraph is OK but the rest of the paragraph is, at best, overlong. There is no real need here to describe the structure and function of the synapse in detail. The next paragraph is very good and would earn good credit. The last paragraph on iproniazid is not wholly accurate. Iproniazid is only a moderately good antidepressant. ECT is not generally used unless absolutely necessary. The rest of that paragraph is good evaluation but is lacking in detail. What are the side effects? Where do tricyclics act? Why do they have fewer side effects?

Overall, the first part of the answer is too descriptive (of which much is not wholly relevant). The evaluation is very limited.

For chlorpromazine the first paragraph is knowledgeable and accurate but is, unfortunately, not relevant. The second paragraph is good but the candidate ought to have indicated where in the brain this overactivity occurs. This could then be mapped onto the behavioural symptoms that are manifest.

The evaluation is again very thin and not entirely accurate. It is only Parkinson's-like symptoms that develop. What are the side effects? Why is tardive dyskinesia not consistent with the dopamine hypothesis (although not wholly relevant, anyway)? What behaviours are changed with the use of the drug? What other drug options are there? Are there non-drug solutions that are side-effect free?

The last paragraph is quite insightful. Unfortunately, the candidate does not tell us what a magic bullet is.

The final mark for this answer is about 8 (description) + 4 (evaluation) = 12/24 (likely to be equivalent to a grade C at A level).

KEY RESEARCH SUMMARY

'Neuroendocrine bases of monogamy', Larry J. Zuoxin Wang and Thomas R. Insel in *Trends in Neurosciences* (1998) 21(2), 71–5.

Article notes

This is a recent review article which shows how two endocrine hormones might play a role in the behaviours that are associated with monogamy. The research is based on work with voles and so you need to consider how relevant the data might be for human monogamous behaviour. Nevertheless, the article illustrates the importance of neuroendocrine control in sexual behaviour. There are some technical details in the article which are not summarised here.

Summary

Monogamy is found in around 3 per cent of mammals, with a higher percentage found in primates. It is defined by an adult male and female pair sharing a nest, preferential copulating with the mate, male parental care and vigorous defending of the nest. Monogamy is contrasted with polygamy and promiscuity.

Voles make a good genus to study in this area as some species, like the prairie vole, are monogamous and some, like the montane vole, are promiscuous. Investigations of neural hormones linked to monogamy have implicated two neuroendocrine hormones, oxytocin (OT) and vasopressin (AVP).

It is well known that OT and AVP control a number of social behaviours in rodents. For example, OT released in the brain at birth could facilitate nurturing behaviour in female rats. Similarly, in hamsters AVP plays a role in the expression of territorial aggression in males. Both of these are component behaviours of monogamy.

It seems that intense mating in the prairie vole stimulates OT release in the female and facilitates social attachment to her mate. The OT release is both necessary and sufficient for such mate preference. In the male prairie vole, mating also leads to partner preference and also to paternal behaviour. However, for males it is not OT but AVP that leads to such behaviours. Indeed, administration of AVP to males facilitates partner preference, aggression towards strangers and parental care. An AVP antagonist blocks these behaviours even in males experiencing extended mating bouts.

The exact mechanism of this neuroendocrine control is uncertain. There are no sex differences in the distribution of OT and AVP receptors. However, there are sex differences in the number of AVP fibres in the lateral septum.

There are neuroendocrine differences between prairie and montane voles that point towards their differences in sexual behaviour. Infusion of AVP in male prairie voles increases aggression towards intruders whereas this does not happen after infusion of AVP in male montane voles. It seems that the two species respond differently to the hormone. Furthermore, the location of the receptors in the prairie vole give some clues as to the cognitive mechanisms involved in monogamy. In prairie voles there are large numbers of OT receptors in the reward areas of the brain whereas in montane voles there are not. Perhaps, then, the OT release in the female is rewarding and leads to conditioning of the female to the smell of her mate.

The article concludes, therefore, that prairie voles are monogamous because of their regional sensitivity to endogenous OT and AVP.

Glossary

The first occurence of each of these terms is highlighted in **bold** type in the main text.

−70 millivolts This is the resting membrane potential.

absorptive phase The period after eating when food is being digested.

acetylcholine A neurotransmitter substance that is released at many brain and peripheral sites.

action potential The wave of ionic changes that travel down an axon when it fires.

adipose tissue A form of body fat.

adrenocorticotropic hormone (ACTH) A hormone that causes the adrenal cortex to release adrenocorticoids.

adrenal cortex The outer layer of the adrenal gland.

adrenal glands The endocrine glands that lie above the kidneys.

adrenal medulla The inner portion of the adrenal gland.

adrenaline A hormone secreted by the adrenal gland.

adrenocorticoids Hormones secreted by the adrenal cortex.

afferent Any neuronal pathway that travels from the periphery towards the brain.

agonist Any drug that causes the same effect as the naturally occurring neurotransmitter substance.

alcohol   A depressant drug.

aldosterone   A mineralocorticoid produced by the adrenal cortex.

amphetamine   One of the stimulant drugs.

analgesic   Any drug that reduces pain.

anandamide   An endogenous substance that acts on the same receptors as cannabis.

androgens   The group name for the male sex hormones.

antagonist   Any drug that prevents the effect of the naturally occurring neurotransmitter substance.

anterior   Frontmost (towards the head end).

anterior nucleus   The part of the hypothalamus that controls the parasympathetic nervous system.

anterior pituitary   The part of the pituitary gland that lies toward the front. This is under hormonal influence from the hypothalamus.

antidepressant   Any drug that relieves the symptoms of depression.

antidiuretic hormone (ADH)   A hormone secreted by the posterior pituitary gland that regulates water balance.

antipsychotic (tranquilliser)   One of the classes of psychoactive drugs that reduce psychosis.

anxiolytic   A drug that reduces anxiety.

arginine vasopressin (AVP)   Another name for antidiuretic hormone.

autonomic nervous system (ANS)   Part of the peripheral nervous system. This is involved in maintaining the level of activity in vital systems depending on the current external circumstances.

autoreceptor   A receptor on the presynaptic terminal that monitors how much neurotransmitter is being released.

axon   The output end of a neuron.

axon hillock   The place on the axon where an action potential is generated.

axonal ending   The ending of an axon including the terminal bouton.

barbiturate   A subclass of depressant drug.

basal ganglia   Part of the brain system for motor control.

behavioural tolerance   Tolerance to a drug that relates to a particular regular behaviour.

benzodiazepine   A subclass of depressant drug.

bipolar depression   Depression that manifests itself as alternating periods of depression and mania.

blood–brain barrier   The barrier that prevents some potentially harmful substances from entering the brain.

brainstem   The part of the brain remaining when the cerebellum and both cerebrum are removed.

Broca's area   An area of the left frontal cortex involved in speech production.

caffeine   A type of stimulant drug.

capillaries   The thinnest form of blood vessels.

catecholamine   The group name for a specific set of neurotransmitters that have a similar molecular shape. They include dopamine and noradrenaline.

caudal   Towards the tail end.

celiac ganglion   One of the ganglia of the sympathetic nervous system.

cell body   The part of an axon in which neurotransmitter is synthesised.

central nervous system (CNS)   The brain and the spinal cord.

central sulcus   A groove visible from the top of the cortex.

cerebellum   Part of the hindbrain. The cerebellum is a structure involved in motor control.

cerebral cortex   The outer 6 mm of the cerebrum.

cerebral hemispheres   The two halves of the forebrain that are separated by the corpus callosum.

cerebral lobes   The four divisions of the cerebral hemispheres.

chlorpromazine   An antipsychotic tranquilliser.

cholecystokinin (CCK)   An intestinal hormone.

cocaine   A stimulant drug.

computerised axial tomography (CAT or CT)   A type of brain scan.

conditioning   Various forms of associative learning: that is, the association of two or more events as being connected. The two main forms of conditioning are classical conditioning and operant conditioning.

contralateral   The other side of the body.

core body temperature   The temperature of our internal organs.

coronal section   A section that is in the plane of the ears.

corpus callosum   The connecting band of nerve fibres that join the left and right cerebral hemispheres.

corpus luteum   The name given to a follicle after it has released an ovum.

correctional mechanism A homeostatic mechanism that helps to maintain the balance of the internal environment.

cortex The topmost 6 mm of the human brain.

corticotrophin-releasing hormone (CRH) Causes the adrenal cortex to release some of its hormones.

cortisol A hormone secreted by the adrenal cortex.

cross-tolerance Tolerance for one drug that is produced by excessive use of another drug.

cytoplasm The fluid on the inside of a cell.

dementia The name given to senility. A loss of intellectual functioning.

dendrite The input ends of a neuron.

dependence The reliance that comes to be placed on some psychoactive drugs.

depressant A class of psychoactive drug.

depression A clinical state of lethargy and tiredness.

detector The means by which imbalances in a homeostatic mechanism are monitored.

diazepam A minor tranquilliser also known as valium.

diencephalon A region of the forebrain containing a number of separate structures.

disinhibition The reversing of an inhibition.

divergence The growing apart of two or more things.

dopamine A classical catecholamine neurotransmitter.

dopamine hypothesis Term usually used to refer to the hypothesis that schizophrenia is the result of an excess of dopamine in the brain.

dorsal Towards the back (as opposed to towards the stomach).

drug dependence The inability to cope without a particular drug.

drug tolerance The lessening effect of a drug with extended use.

dura mater The membrane that separates the brain from the skull.

efferent Any neuronal pathway that travels from the brain to the periphery.

electroconvulsive therapy (ECT) A treatment of shocks used to relieve certain kinds of depression.

electroencephalograph (EEG) Brain waves recorded from the surface of the skull.

electron microscope A microscope that enables scientists to view the smallest details of neurons.

end organ   An organ that is innervated by an efferent nerve.

endocrine system   The hormonal system.

endogenous depression   Depression due to some form of clinical disorder.

endorphin   An endogenous opiate neurotransmitter.

enkephalin   An endogenous opiate neurotransmitter.

enzyme   A substance that causes molecules to be formed or broken apart.

excitatory   Stimulating.

extracellular fluid   The fluid that lies between cells (i.e. in the extracellular spaces).

fasting phase   The period of time between the finish of digesting one meal and the eating of another one.

fatty acids   The product of the breakdown of fat in the liver.

feedback mechanism   A mechanism by which the release of a chemical has a regulatory role on any subsequent release.

fight or flight   A state in which an organism has to decide either to fight an opponent or run away. This involves sympathetic nervous system activity.

firing   Carrying one or more action potentials.

follicle-stimulating hormone (FSH)   A sex hormone released by the anterior pituitary gland.

forebrain   The brain region that includes (among others) the cerebral hemispheres. It is the newest brain region in evolutionary terms.

frontal lobe   One of the four lobes of the cerebral hemispheres. It lies at the front of the human brain.

functional deficit   Typically the word function in this phrase refers to a cognitive process. Hence the term implies an inability to perform one or more cognitive processes (e.g. memory, perception, language processing, etc).

GABA   A classical neurotransmitter substance. Usually has an inhibitory action.

ganglion/ganglia   A densely packed collection of neuronal cell bodies. Ganglia is the plural term.

general anaesthesia   A consequence of an excess of a sedative hypnotic.

glands   Organs that secrete hormones directly into the blood.

glucagon   A hormone that breaks down stored fat to provide usable energy.

glucocorticoids   A group of hormones from the adrenal cortex that raise the amount of usable energy.

glucose   The body's major fuel for producing energy.

glucostatic hypothesis   The suggestion that hunger is initiated by a lack of available glucose.

glycerol   A product of the breakdown of fat in the liver.

glycogen   The fat that glucose is converted into by the liver.

gonadotrophin-releasing hormone (GnRH)   A hypothalamic hormone that causes the anterior pituitary to release its sex hormones.

growth hormone   A hormone that is responsible for promoting growth.

haloperidol   A high-potency antipsychotic drug.

hindbrain   The area where the brain meets the spinal cord. It is the oldest part of the brain in evolutionary terms.

hippocampus   A structure of the forebrain that is involved in memory and emotion.

homeostasis   The maintenance of the body's internal environment.

horizontal section   A section through the brain taken horizontal to the ground.

hormone   A substance that helps to regulate the internal environment.

hunger mechanism   Any process that leads to the search for food.

hypnosis   One of the states that can be attained when taking sedative hypnotic drugs.

hypothalamus   A structure of the forebrain that plays a role in regulating a number of vital functions such as the release of hormones.

inferior colliculus   An auditory processing structure of the brainstem.

information processing   The system by which different parts of the brain can organise and interpret information coming in to them. The means by which they do this are referred to as processes.

inhibitory   Preventing stimulation.

insulin   A hormone that helps the body to store excess energy sources as fat.

intracellular fluid   The fluid inside a cell.

ion   A charged atom.

iproniazid   An example of an MAOI antidepressant.

ipsilateral   Same side of the body.

ischymetric hypothesis   The suggestion that hunger is the result of changes in the rate of metabolism.

isotonic   Of equal osmotic pressure.

lateral   Away from the midline.

lateral hypothalamus   A nucleus of the hypothalamus involved in the mechanisms of hunger.

light microscope   The microscope available before the invention of the electron microscope. This is the conventional microscope.

limbic system   A system of brain structures that includes the hippocampus. This system plays an important role in emotion.

lipostatic theory   The suggestion that hunger is induced by the detection of fats being broken down to provide energy once the available glucose has been used up.

lithium (salts/carbonate)   A drug used to treat manic-depression.

lobotomy   The surgical removal of all or part of a cerebral lobe.

luteinising hormone   One of the female sex hormones.

lysergic acid diethylamide (LSD)   A psychedelic drug.

magnetic resonance imaging (MRI)   A brain-scanning technique.

major tranquilliser   The general term used for depressants.

manic depression   A condition in which states of mania and depression alternate.

marijuana   A psychedelic drug.

medial   Towards the midline.

medulla oblongata   A structure in the hindbrain.

menstruation   The periodic discharge of blood and part of the uterine wall in mature women.

mescaline   A psychedelic drug.

metabolism   The utilisation of energy.

microelectrode   A very small electrode used to record from one or a few neurons.

micropipette   A very small pipette capable of delivering just a few molecules of a substance through its tip.

midbrain   The region of the brain between the forebrain and the hindbrain. It includes the superior and inferior colliculi.

mineralocorticoid   One type of hormone secreted by the adrenal cortex.

modality   A sense.

monoamine oxidase A chemical that helps to break down the monoamine neurotransmitters (i.e. noradrenaline, dopamine and serotonin).

monoamine oxidase inhibitors (MAOIs) A type of antidepressant drug.

motor cortex An area of the cerebral cortex that initiates voluntary movement.

multiple unit activity (MUA) The recording from more than one neuron.

myelin (sheath) The insulating layer around most axons.

narcotic Another name for an opiate.

negative feedback A self-regulating system whereby if A causes the release of B then the presence of B prevents the release of A.

negative symptoms One group of the symptoms of schizophrenia. Typically, they include flattened emotion.

nerve (fibre) A collection of neurons that run along the same course.

neurohormonal A combination of neuronal and hormonal control.

neuroleptic Another name for an antipsychotic drug.

neuron The functional unit of the nervous system.

neuronal membrane The membrane surrounding a neuron across which ion exchange can occur.

neurotransmitter (substance) A chemical that is released from the terminal bouton of a neuron in response to an action potential.

nicotine A stimulant drug.

node of Ranvier The periodic gap in the myelin sheath that surrounds most neurons.

noradrenaline A monoamine neurotransmitter substance.

noradrenergic Involving noradrenaline.

nucleus/nuclei A structure containing a large number of densely packed neuronal cell bodies.

occipital lobe One of the four lobes of the cerebral hemispheres. It lies at the back of the human brain.

oestrogen A female sex hormone secreted by the ovaries.

osmotic thirst Thirst resulting from a lack of water inside cells.

ovulation The release of an ovum from the ovary.

oxytocin A posterior pituitary hormone involved in contractions of the uterus and lactation.

parasympathetic nervous system A branch of the autonomic nervous system.

paraventricular nucleus   One of the nuclei of the hypothalamus that send axons to the posterior pituitary gland.

parietal lobe   One of the four lobes of the cerebral hemispheres. It lies at the top of the human brain.

Parkinson's disease   A motor disease of the basal ganglia.

peripheral nervous system (PNS)   The part of the nervous system outside the brain and spinal cord.

pharmacodynamic tolerance   Tolerance to a drug that is the result of the liver metabolising the drug more quickly.

phenothiazines   A class of antipsychotic drugs.

physiological dependence   The need to keep taking a substance because of the physical effects of withdrawal.

physostigmine   A type of hallucinogenic drug.

piloerection   The erection of hairs on the skin due to cold.

pituitary gland   The gland in the brain that controls the hormonal function of many of the peripheral glands. It is often called the 'master gland'.

pituitary stalk   The nerve fibre that joins the hypothalamus to the pituitary gland.

pons   One of the structures of the hindbrain.

positive symptoms   A class of symptoms of schizophrenia. They include delusions and disturbed thoughts.

positron emission tomography (PET)   A type of brain-scanning technique.

posterior   Towards the tail end.

posterior nucleus   A hypothalamic nucleus that controls the sympathetic nervous system.

posterior pituitary   A region of the pituitary gland.

postsynaptic membrane   The membrane of the receiving neuron in the region of a synapse.

postsynaptic terminal   The area of the postsynaptic membrane that contains the receptor sites.

potency   The strength with which a drug has its effect.

preoptic area/nucleus   An area of the hypothalamus.

progesterone   A female sex hormone secreted by the corpus luteum.

prolactin   A hormone that activates milk release from the mammary glands.

prolactin-inhibiting factor (PIF) A hypothalamic hormone that inhibits the secretion of prolactin from the anterior pituitary gland.

psychoactive drug Any drug that has a psychobehavioural effect.

psychobehavioural Relating to behaviour of the mind.

psychological dependence The inability to cease taking a drug because of a psychological need for it.

raphe nucleus A structure in the hindbrain. It has a role in sleep.

raphe system A system of nuclei in the hindbrain.

reactive depression Non-clinical depression that is the result of an external event.

receptor (site) The points on a neuronal membrane to which a neurotransmitter substance can attach.

releasing hormone A hormone released by the hypothalamus that causes the anterior pituitary gland to release hormones.

reserpine An antipsychotic tranquilliser.

resting membrane potential The voltage across the neuronal membrane when the neuron is not firing an action potential.

reticular formation Part of the hindbrain that is involved in arousal.

rostral Towards the head end.

saggital section A section through the brain cut from front to back.

satiety mechanism A process that leads to the cessation of eating.

schizophrenia A type of psychosis.

sedation Making calm.

sedative hypnotic A class of drugs also known as depressants.

semi-permeable membrane A membrane that lets some substances (e.g. ions) through depending on the local conditions.

serotonergic Involving serotonin.

serotonin A classical neurotransmitter substance.

set point The limited range (point) of conditions over which an internal mechanism can function properly.

single unit activity (SUA) The recording of activity from a single neuron.

somatic nervous system The part of the peripheral nervous system that serves the senses and the muscles.

somatocrinin A hypothalamic hormone that causes the anterior pituitary gland to secrete growth hormone.

somatosensory cortex Part of the cerebral cortex involved in the detection of tactile sensation.

somatostatin A hypothalamic hormone that causes the anterior pituitary gland to stop secreting growth hormone.

spatial summation The cumulative effect of local ion exchanges at different points on the postsynaptic membrane at one moment in time.

spinal cord Part of the central nervous system.

stimulant A class of psychoactive drug.

stimulating hormone A hormone released by the pituitary gland that causes a peripheral gland to release its hormone.

stress A condition under which it is difficult to cope.

subfornical organ A region of the brain involved in drinking.

substantia nigra A structure of the basal ganglia. This is destroyed in Parkinson's disease.

sulci Folds in the cerebral cortex.

superior colliculus A visual processing structure of the brainstem.

supraoptic nucleus One of the nuclei of the hypothalamus that send axons to the posterior pituitary gland.

sympathetic nervous system Part of the autonomic nervous system.

synapse A region including the terminal bouton, the postsynaptic membrane and the synaptic cleft.

synaptic cleft The gap between the presynaptic and postsynaptic membranes.

synaptic vesicle A structure in the terminal bouton that stores neurotransmitter substances.

tardive dyskinesia A motor disease associated with an excess of dopamine.

telencephalon A region of the forebrain.

temporal lobe One of the four lobes of the cerebral hemispheres. It has two parts, one either side of the human brain.

temporal summation The cumulative effect over time of local ion exchanges at one point on the postsynaptic membrane.

terminal bouton The region at the end of an axon.

testosterone A male hormone secreted by the testes.

tetrahydrocannabinol (THC) The active chemical in cannabis.

thalamus A structure in the diencephalon.

thyroid-stimulating hormone (TSH) An anterior pituitary hormone that stimulates the thyroid gland to secrete thyroxine.

thyrotropin-releasing hormone (TRH) A hypothalamic hormone that causes the anterior pituitary gland to secrete thyroid-stimulating hormone.

thyroxine The hormone secreted by the thyroid gland.

tolerance The need for an increasing dosage of a drug to achieve the same psychobehavioural effect.

tricyclic antidepressant A class of antidepressant drugs.

unipolar depression Depression in which that is the only major clinical symptom.

vasoconstriction The constricting of the blood vessels.

ventral The front (or stomach) side.

ventromedial hypothalamus A region of the hypothalamus involved in the control of eating.

vesicle *See* synaptic vesicle.

visual cortex The cortical area of the brain in the occipital lobe involved in visual processing.

volumetric thirst Thirst due to a loss of blood volume.

Wernicke's area An area in the left temporal lobe involved in language comprehension.

Bibliography

Adolph, E.F. (1950) Thirst and its inhibition in the stomach. *American Journal of Physiology*, 161: 374–86.

Auerbach, S.H., Allard, T., Naeser, M., Alexander, M.P. and Albert, M.L. (1982) Pure word deafness: analysis of a case with bilateral lesions and a deficit at the prephonemic level. *Brain*, 105: 271–300.

Berger, T.W., Berry, S.D. and Thompson, R.F. (1986) Role of the hippocampus in classical conditioning of aversive and appetitive behaviours. In: R.L. Isaacson and K.H. Pribram (eds) *The Hippocampus*. Vol. 4. Plenum Press, New York.

Blass, E.M. and Epstein, A.N. (1971) A lateral preoptic osmosensitive zone for thirst in the rat. *Journal of Comparative and Physiological Psychology*, 76: 378–94.

Blass, E.M. and Hall, W.G. (1976) Drinking termination: interactions among hydrational, orogastric, and behavioural controls in rats. *Psychological Review*, 83: 356–74.

Blass, E.M. and Kraly, F.S. (1974) Medial forebrain bundle lesions: specific loss of feeding to decreased glucose utilization in rats. *Journal of Comparative and Physiological Psychology*, 86: 679–92.

Bleuler, E. (1911) *Textbook of Psychiatry*. Translated by A. Brill. New York, Macmillan, 1936.

Brady, J.V., Porter, R.W., Conrad, D.G. and Mason, J.W. (1958) Avoidance behaviour and the development of gastroduodenal ulcers. *Journal of the Experimental Analysis of Behaviour*, 1: 69–72.

Cade, J.F. (1949) Lithium salts in the treatment of psychotic excitement. *Medical Journal of Australia*, 2: 349–52.

Carlson, N.R. (1998) *Physiology of Behaviour*. 6th edn. Allyn & Bacon, Boston, MA. Chapter 5.

Cicero, T.J. (1978) Tolerance to and physical dependence on alcohol: Behavioural and neurobiological mechanisms. In: M.A. Lipton, A. Dimascio and K.F. Killman (eds) *Psychopharmacology*. Raven Press, New York.

Dement, W. and Kleitman, N. (1957) Cyclic variations in EEG during sleep and their relation to eye movements, body motility, and dreaming. *Electroencephalography and Clinical Neurophysiology*, 9: 673–90.

Ellis, L. and Ames, M.A. (1987) Neurohormonal functioning and sexual orientation: A theory of homosexuality-heterosexuality. *Psychological Bulletin*, 101: 233–58.

Epstein, A.N. and Teitlebaum, T. (1962) Regulation of food intake in the absence of taste, smell, and other oropharyngeal sensations. *Journal of Comparative and Physiological Psychology*, 55: 753–9.

Fitzsimmons, J.T. (1971) The hormonal control of water and sodium appetite. In: L. Martini and W.F. Ganong (eds) *Frontiers in Neuroendocrinology*. Oxford University Press, New York.

Fitzsimmons, J.T. and Moore-Gillon, M.J. (1980) Drinking and antidiuresis in response to reductions in venous return in the dog: Neural and endocrine mechanisms. *Journal of Physiology*, 308: 403–16.

Foltz, E.L. and Millett, F.E. (1964) Experimental psychosomatic disease states in monkeys. I. Peptic ulcer – 'executive monkeys'. *Journal of Surgical Research*, 4: 445–53.

Freedman, M. and Oscar-Berman, M. (1986) Bilateral frontal lobe disease and selective delayed response deficits in humans. *Behavioural Neuroscience*, 100: 337–42.

Fuster, J.M. (1958) The effects of stimulation of brain stem on tachistoscopic perception. *Science*, 127: 150.

Geliebter, A., Westreich, S., Hashim, S.A. and Gage, D. (1987) Gastric balloon reduces food intake and body weight in obese rats. *Physiology and Behaviour*, 39: 399–402.

Gibbs, J. (1973) Cholecystokinin decreases food intake in rats. *Journal of Comparative and Physiological Psychology*, 84: 488–95.

Gonzalez, M.F. and Deutsch, J. A. (1981) Vagotomy abolishes cues of satiety produced by gastric distension. *Science*, 212: 1283–4.

Grilly, D.M. (1994) *Drugs and Human Behaviour*. Allyn & Bacon, Boston, MA.

Grossman, S.P., Dacey, D., Halaris, A.E., Collier, T. and Routtenberg, A. (1978) Aphagia and adipsia after preferential destruction of nerve cell bodies in hypothalamus. *Science*, 202: 537–9.

Han, P.W. (1967) Hypothalamic obesity in rats without hyperphagia. *Transactions of the New York Academy of Sciences*, 30: 229–43.

Heninger, G.R. and Charney, D.S. (1987) Mechanism of action of antidepressant treatments: Implications for the etiology and treatment of depression disorders. In: H.Y. Meltzer (ed.) *Psychopharmacology: The Third Generation of Progress*. Raven Press: New York.

Hess, W.R. (1954) *Diencephalon: Autonomic and Extra Pyramidal Functions*. Grune & Startton: New York.

Hoebel, B.G. and Teitelbaum, P. (1966) Weight regulation in normal and hypothalamic hyperphagic rats. *Journal of Comparative and Physiological Psychology*, 61: 189–93.

Holmes, D.S. (1994) *Abnormal Psychology*. 2nd edn. Harper Collins, London.

Hubel, D.H. and Wiesel, T.N. (1977) Functional architecture of the macaque monkey visual cortex. *Proceedings of the Royal Society of London*, B, 198: 1–59.

Janowitz, H.D. and Grossman, M.I. (1949) Some factors affecting the food intake of normal dogs and dogs with esophagostomy and gastric fistula. *American Journal of Physiology*, 159: 143–8.

Jobst, K. (1992) Detection in life of confirmed Alzheimer's disease using a simple measurement of temporal lobe atrophy by computed tomography. *Lancet*, 340: 1179–83.

Jouvet, M. and Renault, J. (1966) Persistent insomnia after lesions of the raphe nuclei in the cat. *Comptes Rendus des Séances de la Société de Biologie*, 160: 1461–5.

Kalat, J.W. (1998) *Biological Psychology*. 6th edn. Brooks/Cole Publishing Company, Belmont, CA.

Kraepelin, E. (1919) *Demetia Praecox*. Translated by R.M. Barclay. Krieger, New York, 1971.

Liebelt, R.A., Bordelon, C.B. and Liebelt, A.G. (1973) The adipose tissue system and food intake. In: E. Stellar and J.M. Sprague (eds) *Progress in Physiological Psychology*. Academic Press, New York.

Mayer, J. (1952) The glucostatic theory of regulation of food intake and the problem of obesity. *Bulletin of the New England Medical Center*, 14: 43.

Mayer, J. (1953) Glucostatic mechanism of regulation of food intake. *New England Journal of Medicine*, 249: 13–16.

Mendelwicz, J. and Ranier, J.D. (1977) Adoption study supporting genetic transmission in manic-depressive illness. *Nature*, 268: 350–60.

Miller, W.R. (1975) Psychological deficit in depression. *Psychological Bulletin*, 82: 238–60.

Nelson, J. and Prosser, C.L. (1981) Intracellular recordings from thermosensitive preoptic neurons. *Science*, 213: 787–9.

Nicholls, J.G., Martin, A.R. and Wallace, B.G. (1992) *From Neuron to Brain*. 3rd edn. Sinauer Associates, Sunderland, MA.

Nicolaïdis, S. (1987) What determines food intake? The ischymetric theory. *NIPS*, 2: 104–7.

Olds, J. (1958) Satiation effects in self-stimulation of the brain. *Journal of Comparative and Physiological Psychology*, 51: 675–8.

Olds, J. and Milner, P. (1954) Positive reinforcement produced by electrical stimulation of the septal area and other regions of the rat brain. *Journal of Comparative and Physiological Psychology*, 47: 419–28.

Papez, J.W. (1937) A proposed mechanism of emotion. *AMA Archives of Neurological Psychiatry*, 38: 725–43.

Pinel, J.P.J. (1998) *A Colorful Introduction to the Anatomy of the Human Brain*. Allyn & Bacon, Boston, MA.

Reber, A.S. (1985) *Dictionary of Psychology*. Penguin Books. London.

Rose, S. (1976) *The Conscious Brain*. Penguin Books, London.

Russek, M. (1971) Hepatic receptors and the neurophysiological mechanisms controlling feeding behaviour. In: S. Ehrenpreis (ed.) *Neurosciences Research*. Vol. 4. Academic Press, New York.

Schneider, A.M. (1995) *Elements of Physiological Psychology*. McGraw Hill, New York.

Schroder, J., Buchsbaum, M.S., Siegel, B.V., Geider, F.J. and Niethammer, R. (1995) Structural and functional correlates of sunsyndromes in chronic schizophrenia. *Psychopathology*, 28: 38–45.

Scoville, W.B. and Milner, B. (1957) Loss of recent memory after bilateral hippocampal lesions. *Journal of Neurology, Neurosurgery and Psychiatry*, 20: 11–12.

Sergent, J. and Signoret, J.L. (1992) Varieties of functional deficits in prosopagnosia. *Cerebral Cortex*, 2: 375–88.

Smith, G.P. and Jerome, C. (1983) Effects of total and selective abdominal vagotomies on water intake in rats. *Journal of the Autonomic Nervous System*, 9: 259–71.

Spinelli, D.H., Jensen, F.E. and DiPrisco, G.V. (1980) Early experience effect on dendritic branching in normally reared kittens. *Experimental Neurology*, 62: 1–11.

Teitelbaum, P. (1955) Sensory control of hypothalamic hyperphagia. *Journal of Comparative and Physiological Psychology*, 48: 156–63.

Index

Coventry University